the Mustard Seed

Jesus asked, "How can I describe the Kingdom of God? What story shall I use to illustrate it? It is like a tiny mustard seed! Though this is one of the smallest of seeds, yet it grows to become one of the largest of plants, with long branches where birds can build their nests and be sheltered."

MARK 4:30-32

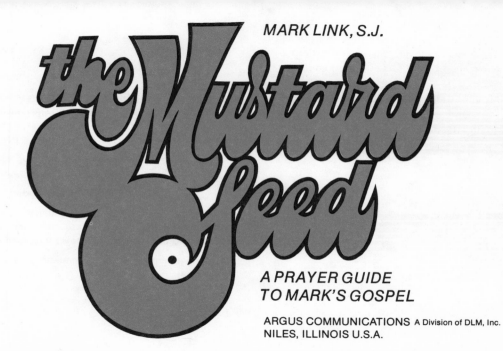

MARK LINK, S.J.

the Mustard Seed

A PRAYER GUIDE TO MARK'S GOSPEL

ARGUS COMMUNICATIONS A Division of DLM, Inc.
NILES, ILLINOIS U.S.A.

Grateful acknowledgment is made to Tyndale House Publishers for permission to reprint scripture quotations from THE WAY—an illustrated edition of THE LIVING BIBLE. Copyright 1973.

Designed by Gene Tarpey

Photography by James Vorwoldt, S.J.
Models: Russ Taylor, Tom Burns, Vito Cece, Craig LaSota.

Argus Communications
A Division of DLM, Inc.
Niles, Illinois 60648 U.S.A.

ISBN: 0-913592-49-8

*Perhaps the only real way
to study the Gospel
is to pray it.*

Contents

Meet Jesus

*I*MAGINE A TEACHER saying: "From now on, follow me! Live as I live. I have no home, no place to lay my head. Neither will you. No questions, no ifs, ands or buts. Follow me!"

No teacher has a right to do that. A teacher teaches: shares knowledge and skill, even shows you how to live. But no teacher has the right to do more than that.

That is why we miss the point of Jesus, if we think of him as only a teacher. Jesus' followers soon learned that Jesus taught not information about life but life.

The gospel is not a book of Jesus' teachings; it is an invitation to life with him. After reading other books, you can say: "That's interesting!" After reading the gospel, you must answer: *yes* or *no*. The gospel is an invitation to life—with an RSVP attached.

Meet Mark

𝒜 CERTAIN YOUNG MAN, dressed only in a linen cloth, was following Jesus. They tried to arrest him, but he ran away naked, leaving the linen cloth behind."

Like a personal "signature," this strange detail ends Mark's report of Jesus' arrest. No other gospel includes it. Some scholars think the "unidentified youth" was Mark, himself.

What brought Mark to the garden that night? Not one of the apostles, perhaps, he was just "out after curfew," unable to sleep. Or, as a young admirer of Jesus, he may have spotted his hero and his friends, and followed them— at a distance.

Mark's full name was John Mark. A Greek-speaking Jew, Mark is referred to in the writings of Peter and Paul. Peter affectionately calls him "Mark, my son" (1, 5:13). Papius, who wrote around 100 A.D., calls Mark the personal interpreter of Peter.

Mark's Gospel

*M*ARK'S GOSPEL is the shortest and the most action-packed. Mark focuses less on what Jesus says and more on what he does.

"This is not to say that Mark's gospel is a song without words. Rather, it is to say that the absence of many words leaves us freer to enjoy the melody which is the person and action of Jesus."

ALEXANDER JONES

In reading Mark, we should stop after each event and ask ourselves: "What does Jesus do?" Then we should ask ourselves: "How do the words of Jesus clarify the meaning of his action—or how do they help us to discover the meaning for ourselves?"

Pray the Gospel

1 Before you begin praying, put yourself in the presence of God
your Father. Ask the Spirit of the Father and Jesus to guide your prayer.

2 Begin by slowly reading the gospel passage. As you do,
put yourself in the shoes of Jesus or one of the gospel figures.
See what they see. Hear what they hear. Experience what they experience.

3 After you have completed your reflection on the gospel passage,
turn to the first paragraph of the prayer-guide. Read it. Ponder it.
Remain with it as long as it holds your prayerful attention.
Do the same with the second paragraph and, finally, the third paragraph.

4 End your prayer period by praying in your own words,
as the Spirit moves you.

5 Finally, jot down in the marginal space—for future reference—
anything that struck you in a special way during your prayer.

Now Begin

𝒩OT FAR from the Dead Sea there's a shallow spot in the Jordan River. From earliest times it has been used as a crossing for caravans from all over the Near East.

On an afternoon, one could see Arabs with white head coverings, Babylonians with rings in their noses, and Ethiopians with their shiny, ebony-colored skin. It was a

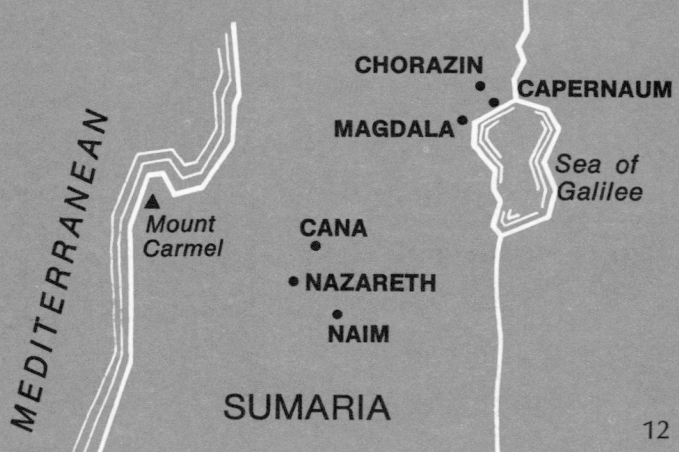

CHORAZIN
CAPERNAUM
MAGDALA
Sea of Galilee
Mount Carmel
CANA
NAZARETH
NAIM
MEDITERRANEAN
SUMARIA

favorite place for people to gather to exchange world news.

One day, however, a new attraction sent people flocking to the shallow crossing. For weeks there were rumors of a strange figure, dressed like the prophets of old, preaching there.

(It is at this point that Mark begins his gospel.)

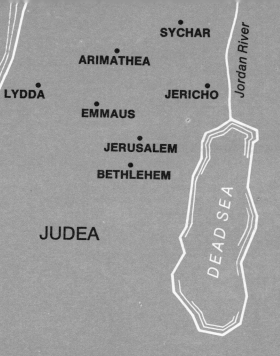

SYCHAR

ARIMATHEA

Jordan River

LYDDA

JERICHO

EMMAUS

JERUSALEM

BETHLEHEM

JUDEA

DEAD SEA

13

JOHN THE BAPTIST

HERE BEGINS THE wonderful story of Jesus the Messiah, the Son of God. In the book written by the prophet Isaiah, God announced that he would send his Son to earth, and that a special messenger would arrive first to prepare the world for his coming.

"This messenger will live out in the barren wilderness," Isaiah said, "and will proclaim that everyone must straighten out his life to be ready for the Lord's arrival."

This messenger was John the Baptist. He lived in the wilderness and taught that all should be baptized as a public announcement of their decision to turn their backs on sin, so that God could forgive them. People from Jerusalem and from all over Judea traveled out into the Judean wastelands to see and hear John, and when they confessed their sins he baptized them in the Jordan River. His clothes were woven from camel's hair and he wore a leather belt; locusts and wild honey were his food.

Here is a sample of his preaching:

"Someone is coming soon who is far greater than I am, so

continued below

prayer guide:

Walk down the dusty road to the Jordan River. Study John closely. Carefully, weigh everything he says.

Into the desert of our lives, there occasionally steps a John the Baptist—someone who speaks to us at a deeper level, someone who opens our eyes to something bigger than ourselves. It may be a friend, an inspiring teacher, or someone who radiates something more than ordinary people. Whoever it is, he points us toward a new star.

The people who walk in darkness
shall see a great Light—a Light that will shine
on all those who live in the land
of the shadow of death.

ISAIAH 9:2

14

much greater that I am not worthy to be his slave. I baptize you with water but he will baptize you with God's Holy Spirit!"

MARK 1:1-8

notes: the death of a friend showed me how short life really is. It let me know that I had to start giving and carring before its to late,

BAPTISM AND TEMPTATION OF JESUS

Then one day Jesus came from Nazareth in Galilee, and was baptized by John there in the Jordan River. The moment Jesus came up out of the water, he saw the heavens open and the Holy Spirit in the form of a dove descending on him, and a voice from heaven said, "You are my beloved Son; you are my Delight."

Immediately the Holy Spirit urged Jesus into the desert. There, for forty days, alone except for desert animals, he was subjected to Satan's temptations to sin. And afterwards the angels came and cared for him.

MARK 1:9-13

Hear the Father's voice split the stillness. See the Son standing in the water. Feel the presence of the Spirit in the air. Hear the scream of the still desert as Jesus enters it. Experience what he does.

Why does Mark begin his gospel with Jesus' baptism rather than his birth? Why does Jesus respond to John's call for repentence and baptism? Why is Jesus tempted?

Praise him for his majestic glory,
the glory of his name.
Come before him clothed in sacred garments.
The voice of the Lord echoes from the clouds.
The God of glory thunders through the skies.
So powerful is his voice; so full of majesty.

PSALM 29:2-4

I fear not having patient with the children at the school not knowing how to react with them

JESUS CALLS FOUR FISHERMEN

Later on, after John was arrested by King Herod, Jesus went to Galilee to preach God's Good News.

"At last the time has come!" he announced. "God's Kingdom is near! Turn from your sins and act on this glorious news!"

One day as Jesus was walking along the shores of the Sea of Galilee, he saw Simon and his brother Andrew fishing with nets, for they were commercial fishermen.

Jesus called out to them, "Come, follow me! And I will make you fishermen for the souls of men!" At once they left their nets and went along with him.

A little farther up the beach, he saw Zebedee's sons, James and John, in a boat mending their nets. He called them too, and immediately they left their father Zebedee in the boat with the hired men and went with him.

MARK 1:14-20

Ponder Jesus' first words as recorded by Mark. Put yourself in the shoes of the first two young men Jesus invited to follow him. What would have been your feelings at the moment?

Simon and Andrew nail a "For Sale" sign on their boat. Zebedee walks to town and posts a "Help Wanted" sign in the marketplace. Four bright young men give up their jobs to follow a strolling preacher. Why did they sacrifice all to do this?

18

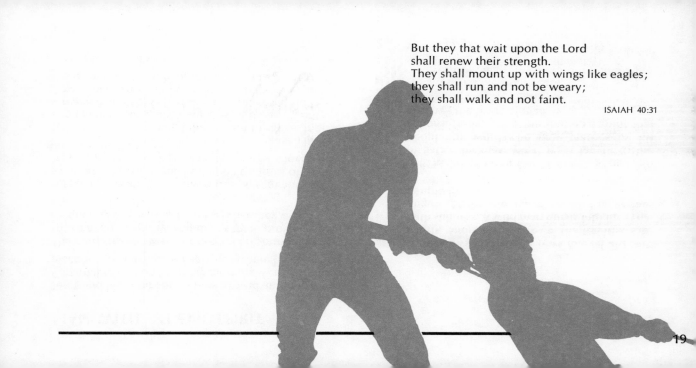

But they that wait upon the Lord
shall renew their strength.
They shall mount up with wings like eagles;
they shall run and not be weary;
they shall walk and not faint.

ISAIAH 40:31

19

MAN WITH AN EVIL SPIRIT

Jesus and his companions now arrived at the town of Capernaum and on Saturday morning went into the Jewish place of worship—the synagogue—where he preached.

The congregation was surprised at his sermon because he spoke as an authority, and didn't try to prove his points by quoting others—quite unlike what they were used to hearing!

A man possessed by a demon was present and began shouting, "Why are you bothering us, Jesus of Nazareth—have you come to destroy us demons? I know who you are—the holy Son of God!"

Jesus curtly commanded the demon to say no more and to come out of the man. At that the evil spirit screamed and convulsed the man violently and left him. Amazement gripped the audience and they began discussing what had happened.

"What sort of new religion is this?" they asked excitedly.

Old Jews and young Jews marvel at Jesus' words. Suddenly a scream shatters the sabbath stillness. A wild man bursts into the synagogue. Share the reactions of the various people involved.

"The kingdom of God is near!"—The reign of Satan declines. What Jesus taught to the people by words, he now teaches by his actions. Jesus expels the irrational spirit that enslaves the heart of man.

He has saved me from death,
my eyes from tears, my feet from stumbling.
I shall live!
Yes, in his presence—here on earth!

PSALM 116:8-9

20

"Why, even evil spirits obey his orders!"

The news of what he had done spread quickly through that entire area of Galilee.

MARK 1:21-28

JESUS HEALS MANY PEOPLE

Then, leaving the synagogue, he and his disciples went over to Simon and Andrew's home, where they found Simon's mother-in-law sick in bed with a high fever. They told Jesus about her right away. He went to her bedside, and as he took her by the hand and helped her to sit up, the fever suddenly left, and she got up and prepared dinner for them!

By sunset the courtyard was filled with the sick and demon-possessed, brought to him for healing; and a huge crowd of people from all over the city of Capernaum gathered outside the door to watch. So Jesus healed great numbers of sick folk that evening and ordered many demons to come out of their victims. (But he refused to allow the demons to speak, because they knew who he was.)

MARK 1:29-34

Simon's front lawn looks like a campsite at sunset. The sick and lame lie on mats and litters everywhere. Hear them call out to Jesus.

Sickness can depress the human spirit. Cured of her fever, Simon's mother-in-law is freed to serve others. Why does Jesus silence the evil spirits? Is it because every man must discover Jesus for himself—apart from what others say?

Lord my God, I pleaded with you,
and you gave me my health again . . .
Then he turned my sorrow into joy!
He took away my clothes of mourning
and gave me gay and festive garments
to rejoice in.

PSALM 30:2, 11

22

JESUS PREACHES IN GALILEE

The next morning he was up long before daybreak and
went out alone into the wilderness to pray.

Later, Simon and the others went out to find him,
and told him, "Everyone is asking for you."

But he replied, "We must go on to other towns as well,
and give my message to them too, for that is why I came."

So he traveled throughout the province of Galilee, preaching
in the synagogues and releasing many from the
power of demons.

MARK 1:35-39

Get up with Jesus. Follow him into the pre-dawn stillness. Share his prayer as he seeks to know his Father's will.

Carl Sandburg wrote: "I go out there and walk and look at the trees and sky. I listen to the sounds of loneliness. I sit on a rock or stump and say to myself, 'Who are you, Sandburg? Where have you been, and where are you going?' "

Tell me where you want me to go
and I will go there.
May every fiber of my being unite
in reverence to your name.
With all my heart I will praise you.
I will give glory to your name forever.

PSALM 86:11-12

JESUS HEALS A LEPER

Once a leper came and knelt in front of him and begged to be healed. "If you want to, you can make we well again," he pled.

And Jesus, moved with pity, touched him and said, "I want to! Be healed!" Immediately the leprosy was gone —the man was healed!

Jesus then told him sternly, "Go and be examined immediately by the Jewish priest. Don't stop to speak to anyone along the way. Take along the offering prescribed by Moses for a leper who is healed, so that everyone will have proof that you are well again."

But as the man went on his way he began to shout the good news that he was healed; as a result, such throngs soon surrounded Jesus that he couldn't publicly enter a city anywhere, but had to stay out in the barren wastelands. And people from everywhere came to him there.

MARK 1:40-45

My heart beats wildly, my strength fails . . .
My loved ones
and friends stay away, fearing my disease.
Even my own family stands at a distance . . .
Don't leave me, Lord; don't go away!

PSALM 38:10-11, 21

Lepers were barred from society. Cures had to be certified by a priest before victims could rejoin the community. Jesus' cure carries a deeper meaning than mere physical healing. There is danger the people will miss it.

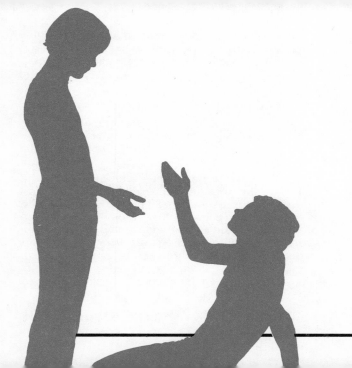

I waited patiently for God to help me;
then he listened and heard my cry.
He lifted me out of the pit of despair,
out from the bog and the mire,
and set my feet on a hard, firm path
and steadied me as I walked along.
He has given me a new song to sing,
of praises to our God . . .

PSALM 40:1-3

JESUS HEALS A PARALYZED MAN

Several days later he returned to Capernaum, and the news of his arrival spread quickly through the city. Soon the house where he was staying was so packed with visitors that there wasn't room for a single person more, not even outside the door. And he preached the Word to them. Four men arrived carrying a paralyzed man on a stretcher. They couldn't get to Jesus through the crowd, so they dug through the clay roof above his head and lowered the sick man on his stretcher, right down in front of Jesus.

When Jesus saw how strongly they believed that he would help, Jesus said to the sick man, "Son, your sins are forgiven!"

But some of the Jewish religious leaders said to themselves as they sat there, "What? This is blasphemy! Does he think he is God? For only God can forgive sins."

Jesus could read their minds and said to them at once, "Why does this bother you? I, the Messiah, have the authority on earth to forgive sins. But talk is cheap—

The crowd grows silent as the mat holding the sick man dangles back and forth in front of Jesus. Experience the paralytic's feelings as he looks into the face of Jesus.

A gasp goes up from the crowd as Jesus speaks the words: "Your sins are forgiven." No Jew in Israel's history ever dared utter these words to a fellow Jew. Shock gives way to awe as the paralytic rises cured. The physical healing confirms the deeper spiritual healing.

anybody could say that. So I'll prove it to you by healing this man." Then, turning to the paralyzed man, he commanded, "Pick up your stretcher and go on home, for you are healed!"

The man jumped up, took the stretcher, and pushed his way through the stunned onlookers! Then how they praised God. "We've never seen anything like this before!" they all exclaimed.

MARK 2:1-12

There was a time
when I wouldn't admit what a sinner I was.
But my dishonesty made me miserable
and filled my days with frustration.
All day and all night
your hand was heavy on me.
My strength evaporated
like water on a sunny day
until I finally admitted all my sins to you
and stopped trying to hide them.
I said to myself,
"I will confess them to the Lord."
And you forgave me! All my guilt is gone.

PSALM 32:3-5

JESUS CALLS LEVI

Then Jesus went out to the seashore again, and preached to the crowds that gathered around him. As he was walking up the beach he saw Levi, the son of Alphaeus, sitting at his tax collection booth. "Come with me," Jesus told him. "Come be my disciple."

And Levi jumped to his feet and went along.

That night Levi invited his fellow tax collectors and many other notorious sinners to be his dinner guests so that they could meet Jesus and his disciples. (There were many men of this type among the crowds that followed him.) But when some of the Jewish religious leaders saw him eating with these men of ill repute, they said to his disciples, "How can he stand it, to eat with such scum?"

When Jesus heard what they were saying, he told them, "Sick people need the doctor, not healthy ones! I haven't come to tell good people to repent, but the bad ones."

MARK 2:13-17

Conversation flows as freely as does the wine. But there is something different about this First Supper. What do the Pharisees fail to see?

Tax collectors worked for the Romans. They bid for their job and would resort to extortion to collect the revenue. Levi didn't fit into conventional categories. The difference between a bold sinner and a great saint is the power of Jesus.

30

You provide delicious food for me
in the presence of my enemies.
You have welcomed me as your guest;
blessings overflow!
Your goodness and unfailing kindness
shall be with me all of my life,
and afterwards I will live with you forever
in your home.

PSALM 23:5-6

QUESTION ABOUT FASTING

John's disciples and the Jewish leaders sometimes fasted, that is, went without food as part of their religion. One day some people came to Jesus and asked why his disciples didn't do this too.

Jesus replied, "Do friends of the bridegroom refuse to eat at the wedding feast? Should they be sad while he is with them? But some day he will be taken away from them, and then they will mourn. (Besides, going without food is part of the old way of doing things.) It is like patching an old garment with unshrunk cloth! What happens? The patch pulls away and leaves the hole worse than before. You know better than to put a new wine into old wineskins. They would burst. The wine would be spilled out and the wineskins ruined. New wine needs fresh wineskins."

MARK 2:18-22

As a boy, Jesus saw new wine ferment, build up a pressure, and burst old storage skins. He also saw new patches shrink and rip bigger holes in the older garments that had been repaired. Listen to Jesus draw upon these images now.

Fasting held a noble place in Israel's worship life. It was a sign of hope and longing—hungering for the Messiah. But should the sign remain when the reality appears? Should not it recede as boyhood does when manhood comes?

We are his sheep and he is our Shepherd.
Oh, that you would hear him
calling you today and come to him!
Don't harden your hearts as Israel did
in the wilderness at Meribah and Massah.
For there your fathers doubted me,
though they had seen
so many of my miracles before . . .

PSALM 95:7-9

QUESTION ABOUT THE SABBATH

Another time, on a Sabbath day as Jesus and his disciples were walking through the fields, the disciples were breaking off heads of wheat and eating the grain.

Some of the Jewish religious leaders said to Jesus, "They shouldn't be doing that! It's against our laws to work by harvesting grain on the Sabbath."

But Jesus replied, "Didn't you ever hear about the time King David and his companions were hungry, and he went into the house of God—Abiathar was High Priest then—and they ate the special bread only priests were allowed to eat? That was against the law too. But the Sabbath was made to benefit man, and not man to benefit the Sabbath. And I, the Messiah, have authority to decide what men can do on Sabbath days!"

MARK 2:23-28

Put yourself in the shoes of Jesus and the disciples. Feel the stinging words of the Pharisee. Weigh carefully Jesus' final sentences to the accusers.

Pharisees were a noble lot. They kept God's law without compromise. But their strength eventually became their weakness. As time passed, they allowed the letter of the law to overshadow its spirit. Laws were made for men, not men for laws.

34

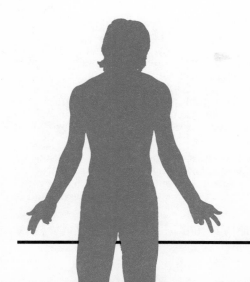

Woe to unjust judges
and to those who issue unfair laws,
says the Lord,
so that there is no justice
for the poor,
the widows and orphans.
Yes, it is true that they even rob the widows
and fatherless children.

ISAIAH 10:1-2

MAN WITH A CRIPPLED HAND

While in Capernaum Jesus went over to the synagogue again, and noticed a man there with a deformed hand. Since it was the Sabbath, Jesus' enemies watched him closely. Would he heal the man's hand? If he did, they planned to arrest him!

Jesus asked the man to come and stand in front of the congregation. Then turning to his enemies he asked, "Is it all right to do kind deeds on Sabbath days? Or is this a day for doing harm? Is it a day to save lives or to destroy them?" But they wouldn't answer him. Looking around at them angrily, for he was deeply disturbed by their indifference to human need, he said to the man, "Reach out your hand." He did, and instantly his hand was healed!

At once the Pharisees went away and met with the Herodians to discuss plans for killing Jesus.

MARK 3:1-6

Stares and whispers broadcast the arrival of Jesus. Sense the brewing storm as Jesus sensed it.

Cautious in opposing Jesus at first, the Pharisees now show their rage openly. Unable to fault Jesus' compassion and good works, the Pharisees challenge his orthodoxy before the law.

36

The Mighty God, the Lord,
has summoned all mankind
from east to west!
God's glory-light shines from the
beautiful Temple on Mount Zion.
He comes with the noise of thunder,
surrounded by devastating fire;
a great storm rages round about him.

PSALM 50:1-3

CROWD BY THE SEASHORE

Meanwhile, Jesus and his disciples withdrew to the beach, followed by a huge crowd from all over Galilee, Judea, Jerusalem, Idumea, from beyond the Jordan River, and even from as far away as Tyre and Sidon. For the news about his miracles had spread far and wide and vast numbers came to see him for themselves.

He instructed his disciples to bring around a boat and to have it standing ready to rescue him in case he was crowded off the beach. For there had been many healings that day and as a result great numbers of sick people were crowding around him, trying to touch him.

And whenever those possessed by demons caught sight of him they would fall down before him shrieking, "You are the Son of God!" But he strictly warned them not to make him known.

MARK 3:7-12

The grotesque parade of lame and sick people is endless. Hear the mounting chorus of calls. Experience the excitement growing.

Faith in Jesus stampedes. Jesus discourages the shouts of those who acclaim him prematurely. Do they have true faith or mere enthusiasm? What if Jesus begins to test the people with trials rather than to shower them with blessings? What then?

38

You commanded the Red Sea to divide,
forming a dry road across its bottom.
Yes, as dry as any desert! . . .
Thus you rescued them from their enemies.
Yet how quickly they forgot again!
They wouldn't wait for him to act,
but demanded better food,
testing God's patience to the breaking point.

PSALM 106:9, 10, 13, 14

39

JESUS CHOOSES TWELVE APOSTLES

Afterwards he went up into the hills and summoned certain ones he chose, inviting them to come and join him there; and they did. Then he selected twelve of them to be his regular companions and to go out to preach and to cast out demons. These are the names of the twelve he chose:

Simon (he renamed him "Peter"),

James and John (the sons of Zebedee, but Jesus called them "Sons of Thunder"),

Andrew,

Philip,

Bartholomew,

Matthew,

Thomas,

James (the son of Alphaeus),

Thaddaeus,

Simon (a member of a political party advocating violent overthrow of the Roman government),

Judas Iscariot (who later betrayed him).

MARK 3:13-19

Jesus studied the faces of the twelve men framed against the evening sky. They had said "yes" to his invitation. Each was different. None knew what lay ahead.

Sir Ernest Shackleton, the polar explorer, put this ad in a London newspaper: "WANTED: Men for hazardous journey — small wages, bitter cold . . . Constant danger, safe return doubtful, honor and recognition in case of success." Over 5000 men applied.

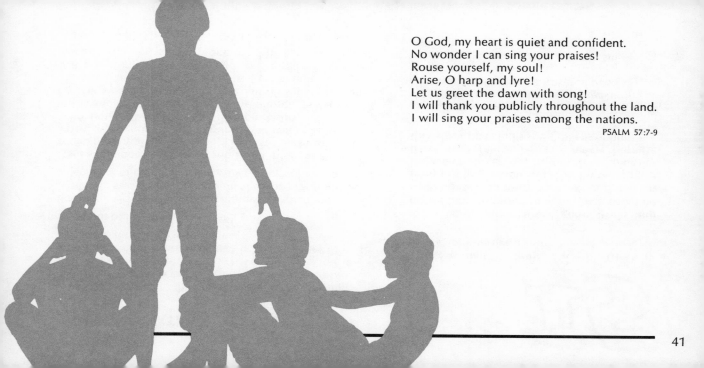

O God, my heart is quiet and confident.
No wonder I can sing your praises!
Rouse yourself, my soul!
Arise, O harp and lyre!
Let us greet the dawn with song!
I will thank you publicly throughout the land.
I will sing your praises among the nations.

PSALM 57:7-9

41

JESUS AND SATAN

When he returned to the house where he was staying, the crowds began to gather again, and soon it was so full of visitors that he couldn't even find time to eat. When his friends heard what was happening they came to try to take him home with them.

"He's out of his mind," they said.

But the Jewish teachers of religion who had arrived from Jerusalem said, "His trouble is that he's possessed by Satan, king of demons. That's why demons obey him."

Jesus summoned these men and asked them (using proverbs they all understood), "How can Satan cast out Satan? A kingdom divided against itself will collapse. A home filled with strife and division destroys itself. And if Satan is fighting against himself, how can he accomplish anything? He would never survive. (Satan must be bound before his demons are cast out), just as a strong man must be tied up before his house can be ransacked and his property robbed.

"I solemnly declare that any sin of man can be forgiven,

"He is mad!" "He has a devil!" These insults stab Jesus like a knife. Feel what he feels.

Forced to admit Jesus' good works and power but too proud to admit they could be wrong, Jesus' opponents attack his character. Jesus can forgive the ignorant; he can forgive the worst sinner. But he can do nothing for those who refuse his forgiveness because they deny that God's spirit dwells in him.

What happiness
for those whose guilt has been forgiven!
What joys when sins are covered over!
What relief
for those who have confessed their sins
and God has cleared their record.

PSALM 32:1-2

42

even blasphemy against me; but blasphemy against the
Holy Spirit can never be forgiven. It is an eternal sin."

He told them this because they were saying he did his
miracles by Satan's power (instead of acknowledging it was
by the Holy Spirit's power).

MARK 3:20-30

JESUS' MOTHER AND BROTHERS

Now his mother and brothers arrived at the crowded house where he was teaching, and they sent word for him to come out and talk with them. "Your mother and brothers are outside and want to see you," he was told.

He replied, "Who is my mother? Who are my brothers?" Looking at those around him he said, "These are my mother and brothers! Anyone who does God's will is my brother, and my sister, and my mother."

MARK 3:31-35

The air crackles with tension. People are starting to polarize in their attitudes toward Jesus. Experience Jesus' inner feelings as he sees this.

Just as groups today, like Pentecostals and Blacks, use the term "brother" and "sister" in the wide sense, so did the ancients of the Near East. Those who do God's will are closer to Jesus than his own blood relatives and friends.

It was not an enemy who taunted me—
then I could have borne it;
I could have hidden and escaped.
But it was you, a man like myself,
my companion and my friend.

PSALM 55:12-13

PARABLE OF THE SOWER

Once again an immense crowd gathered around him on the beach as he was teaching, so he got into a boat and sat down and talked from there. His usual method of teaching was to tell the people stories. One of them went like this:

"Listen! A farmer decided to sow some grain. As he scattered it across the field, some of it fell on a path, and the birds came and picked it off the hard ground and ate it. Some fell on thin soil with underlying rock. It grew up quickly enough, but soon wilted beneath the hot sun and died because the roots had no nourishment in the shallow soil. Other seeds fell among thorns that shot up and crowded the young plants so that they produced no grain. But some of the seeds fell into good soil and yielded thirty times as much as he had planted— some of it even sixty or a hundred times as much! If you have ears, listen!"

MARK 4:1-9

Crowds of people line the rim of the lake. Perched on cliffs and sitting on beaches, they fix their total attention on Jesus.

Parables are stories with deeper meanings: "earthly stories with heavenly meanings," as someone put it. Jesus referred to familiar things to help people discover unfamiliar truths. Like seeds, his words fell into the "soil" of his hearers' hearts. The more open the soil, the greater the understanding.

As the rain and snow
come down from heaven . . .
and cause the grain to grow
and to produce seed for the farmer
and bread for the hungry,
so also is my Word.
I send it out and it always produces fruit . . .
ISAIAH 55:10-11

PURPOSE OF PARABLES

Afterwards, when he was alone with the Twelve and with his other disciples, they asked him, "What does your story mean?"

He replied, "You are permitted to know some truths about the Kingdom of God that are hidden to those outside the Kingdom: 'Though they see and hear, they will not understand or turn to God, or be forgiven for their sins'."

MARK 4:10-12

When the supper hour approaches, most of the people return home. A small group, however, put off the supper to prolong the discussion.

Many people cannot bear to hear truth spoken bluntly. Parables yield up the truth gradually—and gently. Parables, also, test a person's desire to learn the truth. Many people hear only what they want to hear. Parables test how open a person is to truth. They leave a person free—to accept or reject the truth.

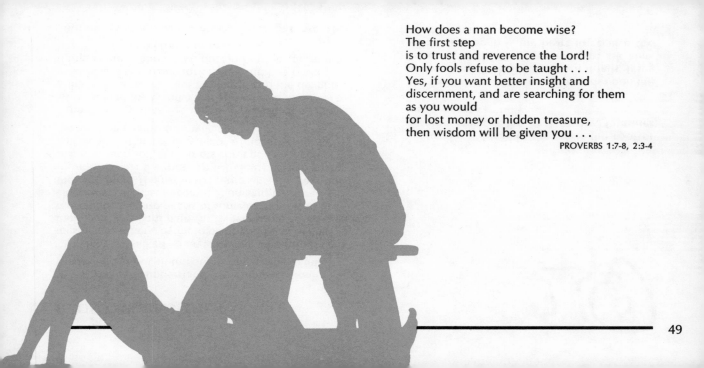

How does a man become wise?
The first step
is to trust and reverence the Lord!
Only fools refuse to be taught . . .
Yes, if you want better insight and
discernment, and are searching for them
as you would
for lost money or hidden treasure,
then wisdom will be given you . . .

PROVERBS 1:7-8, 2:3-4

49

JESUS EXPLAINS THE PARABLE

"But if you can't understand *this* simple illustration, what will you do about all the others I am going to tell?

"The farmer I talked about is anyone who brings God's message to others, trying to plant good seed within their lives. The hard pathway, where some of the seed fell, represents the hard hearts of some of those who hear God's message; Satan comes at once to try to make them forget it. The rocky soil represents the hearts of those who hear the message with joy, but, like young plants in such soil, their roots don't go very deep, and though at first they get along fine, as soon as persecution begins, they wilt.

"The thorny ground represents the hearts of people who listen to the Good News and receive it, but all too quickly the attractions of this world and the delights of wealth, and the search for success and lure of nice things come in and crowd out God's message from their hearts, so that no crop is produced.

"But the good soil represents the hearts of those who

The sky reddens in the west; the cool of evening replaces the heat of day. Consider Jesus' words carefully.

The fruitfulness of the seed depends upon the openness of the soil into which it falls. Jesus draws a parallel. Each person must ask himself: "How open is my heart to receive the words of Jesus?"

truly accept God's message and produce a plentiful harvest for God—thirty, sixty, or even a hundred times as much as was planted in their hearts."

MARK 4:13-20

Oh, the joys of those
who do not follow evil men's advice,
who do not hang around with sinners,
scoffing at the things of God:
But they delight in doing everything
God wants them to,
and day and night are always meditating
on his laws and thinking about ways
to follow him more closely.
They are like trees along a river bank
bearing luscious fruit each season
without fail.
Their leaves shall never wither,
and all they do shall prosper.

PSALM 1:1-3

LAMP UNDER A BOX

Then he asked them, "When someone lights a lamp, does he put a box over it to shut out the light? Of course not! The light couldn't be seen or used. A lamp is placed on a stand to shine and be useful.

"All that is now hidden will someday come to light. If you have ears, listen! And be sure to put into practice what you hear. The more you do this, the more you will understand what I tell you. To him who has shall be given; from him who has not shall be taken away even what he has."

MARK 4:21-25

The Lake grows calm. Soon darkness will settle upon it. This suggests an image to Jesus.

Jesus instructs his followers that they must be a light in the darkness. They have been called. And to those who have been given much, much more is expected. Only to the extent that a person gives of himself can he empty himself to receive more.

If I try to hide in the darkness,
the night becomes light around me.
For even darkness cannot hide from God;
to you the night shines as bright as day.
Darkness and light are both alike to you.

PSALM 139:11-12

PARABLE OF THE GROWING SEED

"Here is another story illustrating what the
Kingdom of God is like:

"A farmer sowed his field, and went away, and as the
days went by, the seeds grew and grew without his
help. For the soil made the seeds grow. First a leaf-blade
pushed through, and later the wheat-heads formed
and finally the grain ripened, and then the farmer came
at once with his sickle and harvested it."

MARK 4:26-29

**The sun begins to slip below the horizon.
Jesus returns to the image of the seed as he
continues his instruction.**

**The kingdom of God is the spirit of God
alive in the hearts of men. This kingdom will
come about without fanfare. Silently—almost
by surprise—the Holy Spirit will bring about
the day of harvest.**

The Lord will show
the nations of the world his justice;
all will praise him.
His righteousness shall be like a budding tree,
or like a garden in early spring,
full of young plants springing up everywhere.

ISAIAH 61:11

PARABLE OF THE MUSTARD SEED

Jesus asked, "How can I describe the Kingdom of God?
What story shall I use to illustrate it? It is like a tiny
mustard seed! Though this is one of the smallest of seeds,
yet it grows to become one of the largest of plants,
with long branches where birds can build their nest
and be sheltered."

He used many such illustrations to teach the people
as much as they were ready to understand. In fact, he
taught only by illustrations in his public teaching, but
afterwards, when he was alone with his disciples,
he would explain his meaning to them.

MARK 4:30-34

**A sprinkling of early stars trumpet the
arrival of night. Except for a few waves lap-
ping the shore, the only sound is that of Jesus'
voice.**

**Reflective children sometimes ask: "How
can God pack a big tree into a tiny seed?"
This image parallels the handful of sleepy men
encircling Jesus on the beach. From them a
transformed world will emerge.**

Praise him for the growing fields,
for they display his greatness.
Let the trees of the forest rustle with praise.
For the Lord is coming
to judge the nations fairly and with truth!

PSALM 96:12-13

56

STORM AT SEA

As evening fell, Jesus said to his disciples, "Let's cross to the other side of the lake." So they took him just as he was and started out, leaving the crowds behind (though other boats followed). But soon a terrible storm arose. High waves began to break into the boat until it was nearly full of water and about to sink. Jesus was asleep at the back of the boat with his head on a cushion. Frantically they wakened him, shouting, "Teacher, don't you even care that we are all about to drown?"

Then he rebuked the wind and said to the sea, "Quiet down!" And the wind fell, and there was a great calm!

And he asked them, "Why were you so fearful? Don't you even yet have confidence in me?"

And they were filled with awe and said among themselves, "Who is this man, that even the winds and seas obey him?"

MARK 4:35-41

He calls to the storm winds;
the waves rise high.
Their ships are tossed to the heavens
and sink again to the depths;
the sailors cringe in terror.
They reel and stagger like drunkards
and are at their wit's end.

PSALM 107:25-27

The fear of the storm gave way to a greater fear. "Who is this man?" No one can answer this question for another. Each man must respond for himself: "Who is this man?"

58

Then they cry to the Lord in their trouble,
and he saves them.
He calms the storm and stills the waves.
What a blessing is that stillness,
as he brings them safely into harbor!

PSALM 107:28-30

59

A POSSESSED MAN

When they arrived at the other side of the lake a
demon-possessed man ran out from a graveyard, just
as Jesus was climbing from the boat.

This man lived among the gravestones, and had such
strength that whenever he was put into handcuffs and
shackles—as he often was—he snapped the handcuffs from
his wrists and smashed the shackles and walked away.
No one was strong enough to control him. All day long
and through the night he would wander among the
tombs and in the wild hills, screaming and cutting
himself with sharp pieces of stone.

When Jesus was still far out on the water, the man had
seen him and had run to meet him, and fell down
before him.

Then Jesus spoke to the demon within the man and said, "Come out, you evil spirit."

It gave a terrible scream, shrieking, "What are you going to do to me, Jesus, Son of the Most High God? For God's sake, don't torture me!"

"What is your name?" Jesus asked, and the demon replied, "Legion, for there are many of us here within this man."

Then the demons begged him again and again not to send them to some distant land.

Now as it happened there was a huge herd of hogs rooting around on the hill above the lake. "Send us into those hogs," the demons begged.

And Jesus gave them permission. Then the evil spirits came out of the man and entered the hogs, and the entire herd plunged down the steep hillside into the lake and drowned.

continued on next page

The herdsmen fled to the nearby towns and countryside, spreading the news as they ran. Everyone rushed out to see for themselves. And a large crowd soon gathered where Jesus was; but as they saw the man sitting there, fully clothed and perfectly sane, they were frightened. Those who saw what happened were telling everyone about it, and the crowd began pleading with Jesus to go away and leave them alone! So he got back into the boat. The man who had been possessed by the demons begged Jesus to let him go along. But Jesus said no.

"Go home to your friends," he told him, "and tell them what wonderful things God has done for you; and how merciful he has been."

So the man started off to visit the Ten Towns of that region and began to tell everyone about the great things Jesus had done for him; and they were awestruck by his story.

MARK 5:1-20

Stories like *The Exorcist* raise the question of evil. Jesus' power over evil frightens the inhabitants of Gerasene. The healed man is sent to bear witness in places closed to Jesus.

My health is broken and my heart is sick;
it is trampled like grass and is whithered . . .
I am reduced to skin and bones
because of my groaning and despair.
I am like a vulture in a far-off wilderness,
or like an owl alone in the desert.
I lie awake, lonely as a solitary sparrow
on the roof.

PSALM 102:3-7

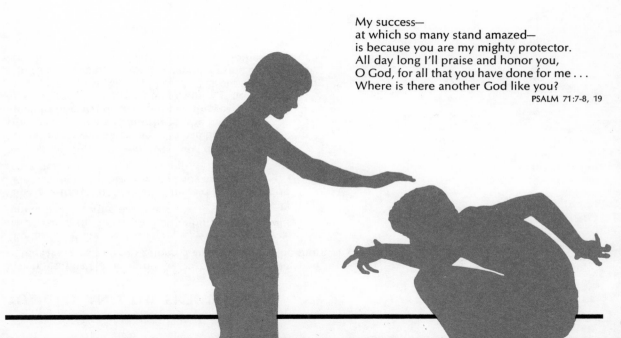

My success—
at which so many stand amazed—
is because you are my mighty protector.
All day long I'll praise and honor you,
O God, for all that you have done for me . . .
Where is there another God like you?

PSALM 71:7-8, 19

63

THE GIRL AND THE SICK WOMAN

When Jesus had gone across by boat to the other side
of the lake, a vast crowd gathered around him on the shore.

The leader of the local synagogue, whose name was
Jairus, came and fell down before him, pleading with
him to heal his little daughter.

"She is at the point of death," he said in desperation.
"Please come and place your hands on her and
make her live."

Jesus went with him, and the crowd thronged behind.
In the crowd was a woman who had been sick for
twelve years with a hemorrhage. She had suffered
much from many doctors through the years and had
become poor from paying them, and was no better but,
in fact, was worse. She had heard all about the wonderful
miracles Jesus did, and that is why she came up behind
him through the crowd and touched his clothes.

For she thought to herself, "If I can just touch his clothing, I will be healed." And sure enough, as soon as she had touched him, the bleeding stopped and she knew she was well!

Jesus realized at once that healing power had gone out from him, so he turned around in the crowd and asked, "Who touched my clothes?"

His disciples said to him, "All this crowd pressing around you, and you ask who touched you?"

But he kept on looking around to see who it was who had done it. Then the frightened woman, trembling at the realization of what had happened to her, came and fell at his feet and told him what she had done. And he said to her, "Daughter, your faith has made you well; go in peace, healed of your disease."

While he was still talking to her, messengers arrived from Jairus' home with the news that it was too late—his daughter was dead and there was no point in Jesus'

continued on next page

65

coming now. But Jesus ignored their comments and said to Jairus, "Don't be afraid. Just trust me."

Then Jesus halted the crowd and wouldn't let anyone go on with him to Jairus' home except Peter and James and John. When they arrived, Jesus saw that all was in great confusion, with unrestrained weeping and wailing. He went inside and spoke to the people.

"Why all this weeping and commotion?" he asked. "The child isn't dead; she is only asleep!"

They laughed at him in bitter derision, but he told them all to leave, and taking the little girl's father and mother and his three disciples, he went into the room where she was lying.

Taking her by the hand he said to her, "Get up, little girl!" (She was twelve years old.) And she jumped up and walked around! Her parents just couldn't get over it. Jesus instructed them very earnestly not to tell what had happened, and told them to give her something to eat.

MARK 5:21-43

Hear Jesus say to the woman: "Your faith has made you well." Feel what Jairus feels as Jesus says: "Don't be afraid. Just trust me."

Jesus looks about and asks: "Who touched me?" Scores of enthusiastic people were reaching out and touching him, but only one person did so with deep faith. Jairus' news of his daughter's death forces his faith to a deeper level.

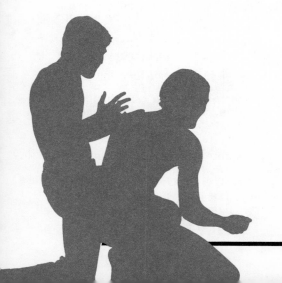

Yes, the Lord hears the good man
when he calls to him for help,
and saves him out of all his troubles.
The Lord is close to those
whose hearts are breaking;
he rescues those
who are humbly sorry for their sins.

PSALM 34:17-18

REJECTED AT NAZARETH

Soon afterwards he left that section of the country and returned with his disciples to Nazareth, his home town. The next Sabbath he went to the synagogue to teach, and the people were astonished at his wisdom and his miracles because he was just a local man like themselves.

"He's no better than we are," they said. "He's just a carpenter, Mary's boy, and a brother of James and Joseph, Judas and Simon. And his sisters live right here among us." And they were offended!

Then Jesus told them, "A prophet is honored everywhere except in his home town and among his relatives and by his own family." And because of their unbelief he couldn't do any mighty miracles among them except to place his hands on a few sick people and heal them. And he could hardly accept the fact that they wouldn't believe in him.

Then he went out among the villages, teaching.

MARK 6:1-6

Walk through the narrow streets of Nazareth with Jesus. See sites that meant a lot to him in his youth. Sense the change of attitude toward him.

In his youth, Jesus appeared on the outside to be like any other boy. But inside him something was happening that eyes could not see. Now it is apparent to all. Some people fear what they see. Some are envious. Others feel threatened. Rejection by old friends is not easy.

You know how they talk about me,
and how they so shamefully dishonor me.
You see them all
and know what each has said.
Their contempt has broken my heart;
my spirit is heavy within me.
If even one would show some pity,
if even one would comfort me!

PSALM 69:19-20

THE DISCIPLES GO FORTH

And he called his twelve disciples together and sent them out two by two, with power to cast out demons. He told them to take nothing with them except their walking sticks—no food, no knapsack, no money, not even an extra pair of shoes or a change of clothes.

"Stay at one home in each village—don't shift around from house to house while you are there," he said. "And whenever a village won't accept you or listen to you, shake off the dust from your feet as you leave; it is a sign that you have abandoned it to its fate."

So the disciples went out, telling everyone they met to turn from sin. And they cast out many demons, and healed many sick people, anointing them with olive oil.

MARK 6:7-13

The mustard seed is ready to be planted. Sense the importance of the moment as Jesus readies the twelve to share his mission with them.

"Don't take anything!" Jesus says. The disciples will have to trust the Father for all their needs. Why? If people don't offer help, is this the sign that they are not open to the message of Jesus? The disciples preach repentance, expel evil, anoint the sick. They share Jesus' own power.

How beautiful upon the mountains
are the feet of those who bring
the happy news of peace and salvation,
the news that the God of Israel reigns.

ISAIAH 52:7

DEATH OF JOHN

King Herod soon heard about Jesus, for his miracles were talked about everywhere. The king thought Jesus was John the Baptist come back to life again. So the people were saying, "No wonder he can do such miracles." Others thought Jesus was Elijah the ancient prophet, now returned to life again; still others claimed he was a new prophet like the great ones of the past.

"No," Herod said "it is John, the man I beheaded. He has come back from the dead."

For Herod had sent soldiers to arrest and imprison John because he kept saying it was wrong for the king to marry Herodias, his brother Philip's wife. Herodias wanted John killed in revenge, but without Herod's approval she was powerless. And Herod respected John, knowing that he was a good and holy man, and so he kept him under his protection. Herod was disturbed whenever he talked with John, but even so he liked to listen to him.

Share Herod's confusion as he hears about Jesus. Flash back with him to that fateful night when he beheaded John.

John was one of the few persons Herod respected. "He liked to listen to him even though he became greatly disturbed every time he heard him." Now, there is Jesus! "Who is he?" Herod, like everyone else, must decide. Not to decide is to decide: "Who is Jesus?"

72

Herodias' chance finally came. It was Herod's birthday and he gave a stag party for his palace aides, army officers, and the leading citizens of Galilee. Then Herodias' daughter came in and danced before them and greatly pleased them all.

"Ask me for anything you like," the king vowed, "even half of my kingdom, and I will give it to you!"

She went out and consulted her mother, who told her, "Ask for John the Baptist's head!"

So she hurried back to the king and told him, "I want the head of John the Baptist—right now—on a tray!"

Then the king was sorry, but he was embarrassed to break his oath in front of his guests. So he sent one of his bodyguards to the prison to cut off John's head and bring it to him. The soldier killed John in the prison, and brought back his head on a tray, and gave it to the girl and she took it to her mother.

When John's disciples heard what had happened, they came for his body and buried it in a tomb.

MARK 6:14-29

My enemies chased and caught me.
They have knocked me to the ground.
They force me to live in the darkness
like those in the grave.
I am losing all hope;
I am paralyzed with fear.
I remember the glorious miracles
you did in days of long ago.
I reach out for you.
I thirst for you as parched land thirsts for rain.
Help me to do your will, for you are my God.
Lead me in good paths,
for your Spirit is good.

PSALM 143:3-5, 10

FEEDS FIVE THOUSAND

The apostles now returned to Jesus from their tour and told him all they had done and what they had said to the people they visited.

Then Jesus suggested, "Let's get away from the crowds for a while and rest." For so many people were coming and going that they scarcely had time to eat. So they left by boat for a quieter spot. But many people saw them leaving and ran on ahead along the shore and met them as they landed. So the usual vast crowd was there as he stepped from the boat; and he had pity on them because they were like sheep without a shepherd, and he taught them many things they needed to know.

Late in the afternoon his disciples came to him and said, "Tell the people to go away to the nearby villages and farms and buy themselves some food, for there is nothing to eat here in this desolate spot, and it is getting late."

But Jesus said, "*You* feed them."

"With what?" they asked. "It would take a fortune to

In a picnic-like setting, the people cluster in groups on the green grass. Suddenly the laughing and talking stop as Jesus raises his eyes upward and begins to pray.

Man gives what little he has. God's creative hand does the rest. Like the tiny mustard seed, the loaves and fishes multiply into a great harvest. To those who believe in Jesus' power over nature, no explanation is needed. To those who don't, none is acceptable.

buy food for all this crowd!"

"How much food do we have?" he asked.

"Go and find out."

They came back to report that there were five loaves of bread and two fish. Then Jesus told the crowd to sit down, and soon colorful groups of fifty or a hundred each were sitting on the green grass.

He took the five loaves and two fish and looking up to heaven, gave thanks for the food. Breaking the loaves into pieces he gave some of the bread and fish to each disciple to place before the people. And the crowd ate until they could hold no more!

There were about 5000 men there for that meal, and afterwards twelve basketsful of scraps were picked up off the grass.

MARK 6:30-44

Oh, that these men would praise the Lord
for his loving-kindness,
and for all of his wonderful deeds!
For he satisfies the thirsty soul
and fills the hungry soul with good . . .
Listen, if you are wise, to what I am saying.
Think about the loving kindness of the Lord!

PSALM 107:8-9, 43

WALKS ON THE WATER

Immediately after this Jesus instructed his disciples to get back into the boat and strike out across the lake to Bethsaida where he would join them later. He himself would stay and tell the crowds good-bye and get them started home.

Afterwards he went up into the hills to pray. During the night, as the disciples in their boat were out in the middle of the lake, and he was alone on land, he saw that they were in serious trouble, rowing hard and struggling against the wind and waves.

About three o'clock in the morning he walked out to them on the water. He started past them, but when they saw something walking along beside them they screamed in terror, thinking it was a ghost for they all saw him.

But he spoke to them at once. "It's all right," he said. "It is I! Don't be afraid." Then he climbed into the boat and the wind stopped!

They just sat there, unable to take it in! For they still

The storm intensifies. The boat begins to take in water. Suddenly a specter begins to move over the waves through the stormy night. Recapture the panic that ensues.

"It is I! Don't be afraid!" The voice of Jesus in the dark silences the wind. The disciples are utterly astounded. How is Jesus' power over the loaves and over the storm connected? Is Jesus performing an "action parable"? What is the deeper meaning of it all?

didn't realize who he was, even after the miracle the evening before! For they didn't want to believe!

MARK 6:45-52

He made the sea and formed the land;
they too are his.
Come, kneel before the Lord our Maker,
for he is our God.
We are his sheep and he is our Shepherd.
Oh, that you would hear him
calling you today and come to him!

PSALM 95:5-7

HEALS THE SICK

When they arrived at Gennesaret on the other side of the lake they moored the boat, and climbed out.

The people standing around there recognized him at once, and ran throughout the whole area to spread the news of his arrival, and began carrying sick folks to him on mats and stretchers. Wherever he went—in villages and cities, and out on the farms—they laid the sick in the market plazas and streets, and begged him to let them at least touch the fringes of his clothes; and as many as touched him were healed.

MARK 6:53-56

Like the morning sun dispelling the darkness, the presence of Jesus lights the world of the sick. See the unfortunates streaming from everywhere.

The people reach out instinctively to touch Jesus. Men sense the need to translate their internal feelings into external acts. The amazement of everyone grows as Jesus cures person after person. They ask one another, "What is all this leading up to?"

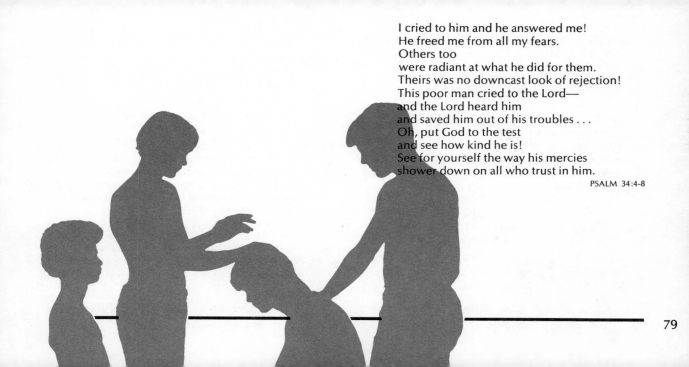

I cried to him and he answered me!
He freed me from all my fears.
Others too
were radiant at what he did for them.
Theirs was no downcast look of rejection!
This poor man cried to the Lord—
and the Lord heard him
and saved him out of his troubles . . .
Oh, put God to the test
and see how kind he is!
See for yourself the way his mercies
shower down on all who trust in him.

PSALM 34:4-8

TEACHING OF THE ANCESTORS

One day some Jewish religious leaders arrived from Jerusalem to investigate him, and noticed that some of his disciples failed to follow the usual Jewish rituals before eating. (For the Jews, especially the Pharisees, will never eat until they have sprinkled their arms to the elbows, as required by their ancient traditions. So when they come home from the market they must always sprinkle themselves in this way before touching any food. This is but one of many examples of laws and regulations they have clung to for centuries, and still follow, such as their ceremony of cleansing for pots, pans and dishes.)

So the religious leaders asked him, "Why don't your disciples follow our age-old customs? For they eat without first performing the washing ceremony."

Jesus replied, "You bunch of hypocrites! Isaiah the prophet described you very well when he said, 'These people speak very prettily about the Lord but they have no love for him at all. Their worship is a farce, for they claim that God commands the people to obey their petty rules.' How right Isaiah was! For you ignore

Leaders with "clean hands" but "unclean hearts" pass judgment on Jesus' disciples. The fire flashes in Jesus' eyes.

Exploiting the poor in the name of religion, prostituting religious worship by making it "all show and no soul"—these abuses bring out the stormy side of Jesus. How awful to be judged a hypocrite by Jesus! Happy the man who never hears this judgment.

You curse and lie,
and vile language streams from your mouths.
You slander your own brother.
I remained silent—you thought I didn't care—
but now your time of punishment has come,
and I list all the above charges against you.

PSALM 50:19-21

80

God's specific orders and substitute your own traditions. You are simply rejecting God's laws and trampling them under your feet for the sake of tradition.

For instance, Moses gave you this law from God: 'Honor your father and mother.' And he said that anyone who speaks against his father or mother must die. But you say it is perfectly all right for a man to disregard his needy parents, telling them, 'Sorry, I can't help you! For I have given to God what I could have given to you.' And so you break the law of God in order to protect your man-made tradition. And this is only one example. There are many, many others."

MARK 7:1-13

WHAT MAKES A PERSON UNCLEAN

Then Jesus called to the crowd to come and hear.
"All of you listen," he said, "and try to understand. Your
souls aren't harmed by what you eat, but by what
you think and say!"

Then he went into a house to get away from the crowds,
and his disciples asked him what he meant by the
statement he had just made.

"Don't you understand either?" he asked. "Can't you
see that what you eat won't harm your soul? For food
doesn't come in contact with your heart, but only
passes through the digestive system." (By saying this he
showed that every kind of food is kosher.)

And then he added, "It is the thought-life that pollutes.
For from within, out of men's hearts, come evil thoughts of
lust, theft, murder, adultery, wanting what belongs to
others, wickedness, deceit, lewdness, envy, slander
pride, and all other folly. All these vile things come from
within; they are what pollute you and make you
unfit for God."

MARK 7:14-23

Though good advice lies deep within a
counselor's heart,
the wise man will draw it out.

PROVERBS 20:5

Man's heart is the "control center" of human action. Dispositions of good and evil germinate in a person's heart like seeds in the soil. Eventually they break through to the surface and bud forth into action.

You deserve honesty from the heart;
yes, utter sincerity and thruthfulness.
Oh, give me this wisdom . . .
Create in me a new, clean heart, O God,
filled with clean thoughts and right desires.
Don't toss me aside,
banished forever from your presence.
Don't take your Holy Spirit from me.
Restore to me again the joy of your salvation,
and make me willing to obey you.

PSALM 51:6, 10-12

A WOMAN'S FAITH

Then he left Galilee and went to the region of Tyre and Sidon, and tried to keep it a secret that he was there, but couldn't. For as usual the news of his arrival spread fast.

Right away a woman came to him whose little girl was possessed by a demon. She had heard about Jesus and now she came and fell at his feet, and pled with him to release her child from the demon's control. (But she was Syrophoenician—a "despised Gentile!")

Jesus told her, "First I should help my own family— the Jews. It isn't right to take the children's food and throw it to the dogs."

She replied, "That's true, sir, but even the puppies under the table are given some scraps from the children's plates."

"Good!" he said, "You have answered well—so well that I have healed your little girl. Go on home, for the demon has left her!"

Desperation is etched on the non-Jewish woman's face as she humiliates herself at the feet of a Jew. Observe her as Jesus tests her sincerity and rewards her faith.

Jesus must minister to the Jews first. They were made ready by the prophets to understand his message. But the woman's lack of preparation is more than made up by her depth of faith. The girl's cure can't be psychological: it occurs at a distance without her knowing how or why.

And when she arrived home, her little girl was lying
quietly in bed, and the demon was gone.

MARK 7:24-30

Who can be compared with God
enthroned on high?
Far below him are the heavens and the earth;
he stoops to look,
and lifts the poor from the dirt,
and the hungry from the garbage dump.

PSALM 113:5-7

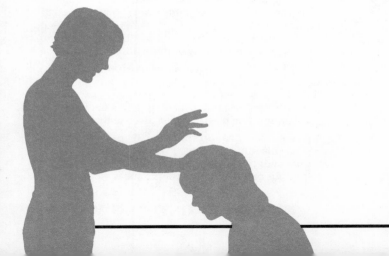

HEALS A DEAF AND DUMB MAN

From Tyre he went to Sidon, then back to the Sea of Galilee by way of the Ten Towns. A deaf man with a speech impediment was brought to him, and everyone begged Jesus to lay his hands on the man and heal him.

Jesus led him away from the crowd and put his fingers into the man's ears, then spat and touched the man's tongue with the spittle. Then, looking up to heaven, he sighed and commanded, "Open!" Instantly the man could hear perfectly and speak plainly!

Jesus told the crowd not to spread the news, but the more he forbade them, the more they made it known, for they were overcome with utter amazement. Again and again they said, "Everything he does is wonderful; he even corrects deafness and stammering!"

MARK 7:31-37

Jesus leads the deaf-mute into a ravine or some similar place of seclusion. Heart pounding, the frightened man wonders what will happen. Experience what it is to be alone with Jesus.

Speaking of the coming of the Messiah, Isaiah said:

Encourage those who are afraid.
Tell them, "Be strong fear not,
for your God is coming to destroy your
enemies. He is coming to save you."
And when he comes,
he will open the eyes of the blind,
and unstop the ears of the deaf.
The lame man will leap up like a deer,
and those who could not speak
will shout and sing!

ISAIAH 35:4-6

I know that you will come
and have mercy on Jerusalem—
and now is the time to pity her—
the time you promised help . . .
I am recording this so that future generations
will also praise the Lord
for all that he has done.
And a people that shall be created
shall praise the Lord.

PSALM 102:13, 18

87

FEEDS FOUR THOUSAND

One day about this time as another great crowd
gathered, the people ran out of food again. Jesus called
his disciples to discuss the situation.

"I pity these people," he said, "for they have been here
three days and have nothing left to eat. And if I send
them home without feeding them, they will faint
along the road! For some of them have come
a long distance."

"Are we supposed to find food for them here in the
desert?" his disciples scoffed.

"How many loaves of bread do you have?" he asked.

"Seven," they replied. So he told the crowd to sit down
on the ground. Then he took the seven loaves,
thanked God for them, broke them into pieces and
passed them to his disciples; and the disciples placed them
before the people. A few small fish were found, too,
so Jesus also blessed these and told the disciples
to serve them.

And the whole crowd ate until they were full, and

**Hungry people stare at Jesus as he takes the
loaves, blesses them, breaks them, and gives
them to his disciples. What does all this mean?**

**The biblical word desert refers not to
Sahara-like sands but to rock-littered land
unfit for farming or grazing. A miracle like this
occurred where the grass was green. Jesus'
ritual is identical to the previous one. The
stress now seems to be on the "bread."**

He commanded the skies to open—
he opened the windows of heaven—
and rained down manna for their food.
He gave them bread from heaven!
They ate angel's food!
He gave them all that they could hold.

PSALM 78:23-25

88

afterwards he sent them home. There were about 4,000 people in the crowd that day and when the scraps were picked up after the meal, there were seven very large basketsful left over!

Immediately after this he got into a boat with his disciples and came to the region of Dalmanutha.

MARK 8:1-10

PHARISEES ASK FOR A MIRACLE

When the local Jewish leaders learned of his arrival they came to argue with him.

"Do a miracle for us," they said. "Make something happen in the sky. Then we will believe in you."

He sighed deeply when he heard this and he said, "Certainly not. How many more miracles do you people need?"

So he got back into the boat and left them, and crossed to the other side of the lake.

MARK 8:11-13

Jesus studies the faces of the men approaching him. What does he see? What do the men approaching see in Jesus' face?

The Pharisees started to argue. They wanted to trap Jesus. Possessing deep insight into human motivation, Jesus could sense disbelief. Trying to search for truth with unbelieving people is like trying to carry water in a net. Jesus refuses to be put on the offensive: was he on trial, or were the Pharisees?

They murder widows, immigrants, and
orphans for "The Lord isn't looking," they
say, "and besides, he doesn't care."
Fools! Is God deaf and blind—
he who makes ears and eyes?
He punishes the nations—
won't he also punish you?
He knows everything—
doesn't he also know what you are doing?

PSALM 94:7-10

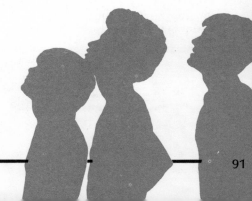

YEAST OF THE PHARISEES

But the disciples had forgotten to stock up on food
before they left, and had only one loaf of bread in the boat.

As they were crossing, Jesus said to them very solemnly,
"Beware of the yeast of King Herod and of the Pharisees."

"What does he mean?" the disciples asked each other.
They finally decided that he must be talking about their
forgetting to bring bread.

Jesus realized what they were discussing and said,
"No, that isn't it at all! Can't you understand? Are your
hearts too hard to take it in? 'Your eyes are to see
with—why don't you look? Why don't you open your ears
and listen?' Don't you remember anything at all?

"What about the 5,000 men I fed with five loaves of
bread? How many basketsful of scraps did you
pick up afterwards?"

"Twelve," they said.

"And when I fed the 4,000 with seven loaves,
how much was left?"

The waves slap lazily against the boat.
After a few miles, someone suggests breaking
out the food. Try to vividly picture the situation.

Were the disciples no better than the Pharisees — trying to get Jesus to work another
miracle? Jesus unreels a series of questions
—trying to get his disciples to probe more
deeply into the meaning of the miracle of
the loaves. Faith is not a question of seeing
more signs, but seeing beyond the signs to
the deeper reality.

"Seven basketsful," they said.

"And yet you think I'm worried that we have no bread?"

MARK 8:14-21

On that day you will say,
'Praise the Lord! . . .
See God has come to save me!
I will trust and not be afraid . . .
Tell the world of his wondrous love.
How mighty he is!'
Sing to the Lord,
for he has done wonderful things.
Make known his praise around the world . . .
For great and mighty is the Holy One
of Israel, who lives among you.

ISAIAH 12:1-6

HEALS A BLIND MAN

When they arrived at Bethsaida, some people brought
a blind man to him and begged him to touch and heal him.
Jesus took the blind man by the hand and led him
out of the village, and spat upon his eyes, and
laid his hands over them.

"Can you see anything now?" Jesus asked him.

The man looked around. "Yes!" he said, "I see men!
But I can't see them very clearly; they look like tree
trunks walking around!"

Then Jesus placed his hands over the man's eyes again
and as the man stared intently, his sight was completely
restored, and he saw everything clearly, drinking in
the sights around him.

Jesus sent him home to his family. "Don't even go back
to the village first," he said.

MARK 8:22-26

Thoughts tumble wildly in the blind man's
mind: "Where is Jesus leading me?" Relive
the blind man's experience—before, during,
and after the cure.

As in the case of the deaf mute, Jesus takes
the man off alone. Similarly personal touch
plays a key role. Sight comes by stages: first
confusion, then clarity. Are these the same
stages Jesus follows in healing the faith-
blindness of people today?

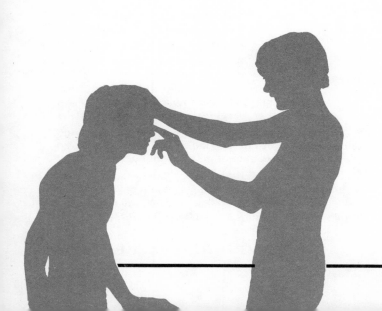

He lets me rest in the meadow grass
and leads me beside the quiet streams.
He restores my failing health.
He helps me do what honors him the most.
Even when walking
through the dark valley of death
I will not be afraid,
for you are close beside me,
guarding, guiding all the way.

PSALM 23:2-4

95

PETER'S DECLARATION OF FAITH

Jesus and his disciples now left Galilee and went out to the villages of Caesarea Philippi. As they were walking along he asked them, "Who do the people think I am? What are they saying about me?"

"Some of them think you are John the Baptist," the disciples replied, "and others say you are Elijah or some other ancient prophet come back to life again."

Then he asked "Who do you think I am?" Peter replied, "You are the Messiah." But Jesus warned them not to tell anyone!

MARK 8:27-30

Dust trails in the wake of the travelers. Alone and away from the crowds, Jesus brings his disciples to a deeper level of understanding.

Scripture portrays Elijah departing life in a fiery chariot amid a whirlwind. Symbolic or not, this portrayal led to the popular belief that Elijah would return. Popular belief also pictured the Messiah as a powerful political king. Jesus must slowly correct this misconception. Until he does, his identity must remain shrouded in questions.

O Lord,
I will praise you with all my heart,
and tell everyone
about the marvelous things you do.
I will be glad,
yes, filled with joy because of you.
I will sing your praises, O Lord God . . .

PSALM 9:1-2

JESUS FORETELLS HIS DEATH AND HIS RISING

Then he began to tell them about the terrible things he would suffer, and that he would be rejected by the elders and the Chief Priests and the other Jewish leaders—and be killed, and that he would rise again three days afterwards. He talked about it quite frankly with them, so Peter took him aside and chided him. "You shouldn't say things like that," he told Jesus.

Jesus turned and looked at his disciples and then said to Peter very sternly, "Satan, get behind me! You are looking at this only from a human point of view and not from God's."

Then he called his disciples and the crowds to come over and listen. "If any of you wants to be my follower," he told them, "you must put aside your own pleasures and shoulder your cross, and follow me closely. If you insist on saving your life, you will lose it. Only those who throw away their lives for my sake and for the sake of the Good News will ever know what

Jesus stops abruptly as people pour from a village ahead to greet him. His words catch his disciples off balance. Share their confusion.

Many Jews expected the promised Messiah to be another David, who would make Israel a world power among the nations. Jesus takes a giant step forward to correct this false notion. Peter misses the point, but a "new seed" is sown as Jesus speaks to the people.

it means to really live.

"And how does a man benefit if he gains the whole world and loses his soul in the process? For is anything worth more than his soul? And anyone who is ashamed of me and my message in these days of unbelief and sin, I, the Messiah will be ashamed of him when I return in the glory of my Father, with the holy angels."

Jesus went on to say to his disciples, "Some of you who are standing here right now will live to see the Kingdom of God arrive in great power!"

MARK 8:31-38; 9:1

In a vision you spoke to your prophet and said, "I have chosen a splendid young man from the common people to be the king— he is my servant David!
I have anointed him with my holy oil.
I will steady him and make him strong . . .
I will protect and bless him constantly and surround him with my love;
he will be great because of me . . .
He will always have an heir;
his throne
will be as endless
as the days of heaven.

PSALM 89:19-21, 24, 29

THE TRANSFIGURATION

Six days later Jesus took Peter, James and John to the top of a mountain. No one else was there.

Suddenly his face began to shine with glory, and his clothing became dazzling white, far more glorious than any earthly process could ever make it! Then Elijah and Moses appeared and began talking with Jesus!

"Teacher, this is wonderful!" Peter exclaimed. "We will make three shelters here, one for each of you . . ."

He said this just to be talking, for he didn't know what else to say and they were all terribly frightened.

But while he was still speaking these words, a cloud covered them, blotting out the sun, and a voice from the cloud said, "*This* is my beloved Son. Listen to *him*."

Then suddenly they looked around and Moses and Elijah were gone, and only Jesus was with them.

As they descended the mountainside he told them never to mention what they had seen until after he had risen from the dead. So they kept it to themselves, but often

Jesus' glory flashes like lightning. For a split second in time, three privileged men see it. Experience their emotions, pulsing violently between fear and attraction.

Three great events in a row: Peter's confession of faith, Jesus' death-rising prophesy —and now this. The Father's voice witnesses to his son (as at Jesus' baptism). Elsewhere John is called Elijah by Jesus. What began on Mt. Sinai with Moses is fulfilled on Mt. Tabor by Jesus.

talked about it, and wondered what he meant by "rising from the dead."

Now they began asking him about something the Jewish religious leaders often spoke of, that Elijah must return (before the Messiah could come). Jesus agreed that Elijah must come first and prepare the way—and that he had, in fact, already come! And that he had been terribly mistreated, just as the prophets had predicted. Then Jesus asked them what the prophets could have been talking about when they predicted that the Messiah would suffer and be treated with utter contempt.

MARK 9:2-13

His lightning flashes out across the world.
The earth sees and trembles.
The mountains melt like wax
before the Lord of all the earth.
The heavens declare his perfect righteousness; every nation sees his glory.

PSALM 97:4-6

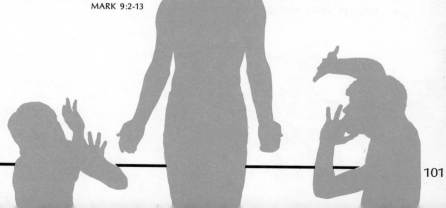

JESUS HEALS A BOY

At the bottom of the mountain they found a great crowd surrounding the other nine disciples, as some Jewish leaders argued with them. The crowd watched Jesus in awe as he came toward them, and then ran to greet him. "What's all the argument about?" he asked.

One of the men in the crowd spoke up and said, "Teacher, I brought my son for you to heal—he can't talk because he is possessed by a demon. And whenever the demon is in control of him it dashes him to the ground and makes him foam at the mouth and grind his teeth and become rigid. So I begged your disciples to cast out the demon, but they couldn't do it."

Jesus said (to his disciples), "Oh, what tiny faith you have, how much longer must I be with you until you believe? How much longer must I be patient with you? Bring the boy to me."

So they brought the boy, but when he saw Jesus the demon convulsed the child horribly, and he fell to the ground writhing and foaming at the mouth.

"How long has he been this way?" Jesus asked the father.

"The crowd watched Jesus in awe." Was there still a trace of the transfiguration left in him?

The father lacks faith: "I do have faith; oh, help me to have more!" The disciples lack power, the kind that comes from God only in prayer. Jesus heals both defects. "He is dead!" But Jesus helped him rise. Could this be a deliberate echo of Jesus' earlier prophecy about his own death and rising?

102

And he replied, "Since he was very small, and the demon often makes him fall into the fire or into water to kill him. Oh, have mercy on us and do something if you can."

"If I can?" Jesus asked. "*Anything* is possible if you have faith."

The father instantly replied, "I *do* have faith; oh, help me to have *more!*"

When Jesus saw the crowd was growing he rebuked the demon.

"O demon of deafness and dumbness," he said, "I command you to come out of this child and enter him no more!"

Then the demon screamed terribly and convulsed the boy again and left him; and the boy lay there limp and motionless, to all appearance dead. A murmur ran through the crowd—"He is dead." But Jesus took him by the hand and helped him to his feet and he stood up and was all right! Afterwards, when Jesus was alone in the house with his disciples, they asked him, "Why couldn't we cast that demon out?"

Jesus replied, "Cases like this require prayer."

MARK 9:14-29

Death stared me in the face—
I was frightened and sad.
Then I cried, 'Lord save me!'
How kind he is! How good he is!
So merciful, this God of ours! . . .
O Lord you have freed me from my bonds
and I will serve you forever.

PSALM 116:3-5, 16

103

JESUS SPEAKS AGAIN ABOUT HIS DEATH

Leaving that region they traveled through Galilee where he tried to avoid all publicity in order to spend more time with his disciples, teaching them. He would say to them, "I, the Messiah, am going to be betrayed and killed and three days later I will return to life again."

But they didn't understand and were afraid to ask him what he meant.

MARK 9:30-32

Jesus takes his disciples off alone—a sign he has something important to say. The disciples are caught unprepared. Share their inner turmoil.

The title "son of man" is the one Jesus preferred. Sixty-nine times it appears in the gospels. Pregnant with meaning, it echoes Daniel's prophecy of the mysterious figure of glory "coming on the clouds of heaven." On the other hand, it points to Jesus' human identification with mankind.

Next I saw the arrival of a Man—
or so he seemed to be—
brought there on clouds from heaven;
he approached the Ancient of Days
and was presented to him.
He was given the ruling power and glory
over all the nations of the world,
so that all people of every language
must obey him.
His power is eternal—it will never end;
his government shall never fall.

DANIEL 7:13-14

105

WHO IS THE GREATEST

And so they arrived at Capernaum. When they were settled in the house where they were to stay he asked them, "What were you discussing out on the road?"

But they were ashamed to answer, for they had been arguing about which of them was the greatest!

He sat down and called them around him and said, "Anyone wanting to be the greatest must be the least— the servant of all!"

Then he placed a little child among them; and taking the child in his arms he said to them, "Anyone who welcomes a little child like this in my name is welcoming me, and anyone who welcomes me is welcoming my Father who sent me!"

MARK 9:33-37

Hear the embarrassing silence that follows Jesus' question. See a small boy with a water-skin enter the room, breaking the stillness and giving water to the dusty, weary travelers.

The serving boy finishes his rounds. He returns to Jesus to see if anything more is needed. Jesus embraces the boy who apparently enjoyed serving as much as the travelers enjoyed drinking. Jesus seizes the incident to teach an important lesson.

Lord, I am not proud and haughty.
I don't think myself better than others.
I don't pretend to "know it all."
I am quiet now before the Lord,
just as a child who is weaned from the breast.
Yes, my begging has been stilled.

PSALM 131:1-2

WHO IS NOT AGAINST US IS FOR US

One of his disciples, John, told him one day "Teacher, we saw a man using your name to cast out demons; but we told him not to, for he isn't one of our group."

"Don't forbid him!" Jesus said. "For no one doing miracles in my name will quickly turn against me. Anyone who isn't against us is for us. If anyone so much as gives you a cup of water because you are Christ's— I say this solemnly—he won't lose his reward.

MARK 9:38-41

This conversation touches many topics. Then John asks Jesus about an incident that has been bothering him. Try to ponder the full meaning of Jesus' words as he answers John.

Whoever helps out another—one in need —does what Jesus came to teach men to do. The spirit of evil (Satan) is the only enemy of Jesus. Between the two there is no middle position. One either serves the Father of Jesus or he does not. Each man is faced with this choice.

Feed the hungry! Help those in trouble!
Then your light
will shine out . . .
and the darkness around you
shall be bright as day.
And the Lord will guide you . . .
and you will be like a well-watered garden,
like an ever-flowing spring.

ISAIAH 58:10-11

TEMPTATIONS TO SIN

"But if someone causes one of these little ones who believe in me to lose faith—it would be better for that man if a huge millstone were tied around his neck and he were thrown into the sea.

"If your hand does wrong, cut it off. Better live forever with one hand than be thrown into the unquenchable fires of hell with two! If your foot carries you toward evil, cut it off! Better be lame and live forever than have two feet that carry you to hell.

"And if your eye is sinful, gouge it out. Better enter the Kingdom of God half blind than have two eyes and see the fires of hell, where the worm never dies and the fire never goes out—where all are salted with fire.

"Good salt is worthless if it loses its saltiness; it can't season anything. So don't lose your flavor! Live in peace with each other."

MARK 9:42-50

No doubt, the serving boy returns with food for the famished travelers. Possibly the smile of innocence on the boy's face prompts Jesus' words.

Man's actions are not neutral. They either serve God's kingdom among men or they do not. Woe to the person whose deeds lead others away from God's kingdom. A man without good deeds is like salt without flavor. He will be cast aside. Woe to such a person!

Though a man
calls himself happy all through his life—
and the world loudly applauds success—
yet in the end he dies like everyone else.
PSALM 49:18-19

111

JESUS TEACHES ABOUT DIVORCE

Then he left Capernaum and went southward to the Judean borders and into the area east of the Jordan River. And as always there were the crowds; and as usual he taught them.

Some Pharisees came and asked him, "Do you permit divorce?" Of course they were trying to trap him.

"What did Moses say about divorce?" Jesus asked them.

"He said it was all right," they replied. "He said that all a man has to do is write his wife a letter of dismissal."

"And why did he say that?" Jesus asked. "I'll tell you why —it was a concession to your hardhearted wickedness. But it certainly isn't God's way. For from the very first he made man and woman to be joined together permanently in marriage; therefore a man is to leave his father and mother, and he and his wife are united so that they are no longer two, but one. And no man may separate what God has joined together."

Later, when he was alone with his disciples in the house, they brought up the subject again.

Like hungry birds in winter flocking around someone with a bag of grain, the people cluster about Jesus. This angers certain Pharisees.

Where Moses gave in, Jesus stands firm. He cites his Father's will clearly expressed in the opening book of the Old Testament. Jesus presents marriage as an act of the creative hand and power of the Father. Only the Father's hand and power can undo it.

He told them, "When a man divorces his wife to marry someone else, he commits adultery against her. And if a wife divorces her husband and remarries, she, too, commits adultery."

MARK 10:1-12

Your laws are my joyous treasure forever. I am determined to obey you until I die.

PSALM 119:111-112

JESUS BLESSES CHILDREN

Once when some mothers were bringing their children to Jesus to bless them, the disciples shooed them away, telling them not to bother him.

But when Jesus saw what was happening he was very much displeased with his disciples and said to them, "Let the children come to me, for the Kingdom of God belongs to such as they. Don't send them away! I tell you as seriously as I know how that anyone who refuses to come to God as a little child will never be allowed into his Kingdom."

Then he took the children into his arms and placed his hands on their heads and he blessed them.

MARK 10:13-16

Children, too small to realize what is going on, are brought to Jesus. The practical-minded apostles think: Let the kids grow up first, then they can come to Jesus if they wish. This isn't Jesus' mind.

Early Christians saw in this event the basis for having their infants baptised into the community of believers. Children are open and trusting. They are an example for anyone who wishes to be touched and blessed by Jesus.

114

O Lord, you alone are my hope;
I've trusted you from childhood.
Yes, you have been with me from birth
and have helped me constantly—
no wonder I am always praising you!

PSALM 71:5-6

RICH MAN

As he was starting out on a trip, a man came running to
him and knelt down and asked, "Good Teacher,
what must I do to get to heaven?"

"Why do you call me good?" Jesus asked. "Only God is
truly good! But as for your question—you know the
commandments: don't kill, don't commit adultery, don't
steal, don't lie, don't cheat, respect your
father and mother."

"Teacher," the man replied, 'I've never once broken a
single one of those laws."

Jesus felt genuine love for this man as he looked at him.
"You lack only one thing," he told him;
"go and sell all you have and give the money to the poor—
and you shall have treasure in heaven—and
come, follow me."

Jesus looks straight at him. The rich man
and Jesus stand face to face. For a moment
neither speaks. What thoughts are in the
minds of each?

"Only God is truly good!" Is Jesus really
asking: Do you believe this is who I am? "It
is easier for a camel. . . ." This ancient figure
of speech illustrates the powerful grip pos-
sessions can have on the human heart. "But
with God everything is possible"—With God's
help, nothing is impossible.

Then the man's face fell, and he went sadly away, for he was very rich.

Jesus watched him go, then turned around and said to his disciples "It's almost impossible for the rich to get into the Kingdom of God!"

This amazed them. So Jesus said it again: "Dear children, how hard it is for those who trust in riches to enter the Kingdom of God. It is easier for a camel to go through the eye of a needle than for a rich man to enter the Kingdom of God."

The disciples were incredulous! "Then who in the world can be saved, if not a rich man?" they asked.

Jesus looked at them intently, then said, "Without God, it is utterly impossible. But with God everything is possible."

Then Peter began to mention all that he and the other disciples had left behind. "We've given up everything to follow you," he said.

continued on next page

Seventy years are given us!
And some may even live to eighty.
But even the best of these years
are often emptiness and pain;
soon they disappear, and we are gone.
Who can realize the terrors of your anger?
Which of us can fear you as he should?
Teach us to number our days
and recognize how few they are;
help us to spend them as we should.

PSALM 90:10-12

And Jesus replied, "Let me assure you that no one has ever given up anything—home, brothers, sisters, mother, father, children, or property—for love of me and to tell others the Good News, who won't be given back, a hundred times over, homes, brothers, sisters, mothers, children, and land—with persecutions!

"All these will be his here on earth, and in the world to come he shall have eternal life. But many people who seem to be important now will be the least important then; and many who are considered least here shall be greatest there."

MARK 10:17-31

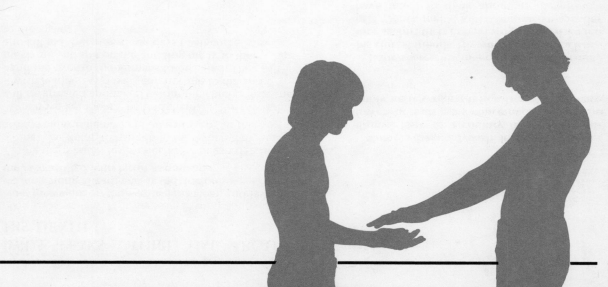

JESUS SPEAKS A THIRD TIME ABOUT HIS DEATH

Now they were on the way to Jerusalem, and Jesus was walking along ahead; and as the disciples were following they were filled with terror and dread.

Taking them aside, Jesus once more began describing all that was going to happen to him when they arrived at Jerusalem.

"When we get there," he told them, "I, the Messiah, will be arrested and taken before the chief priests and the Jewish leaders, who will sentence me to die and hand me over to the Romans to be killed. They will mock me and spit on me and flog me with their whips and kill me; but after three days I will come back to life again."

MARK 10:32-34

Rumors begin. Jewish leaders no longer dismiss Jesus as a country faith-healer. Followers of Jesus grow concerned: "Doesn't he know he is walking into a trap?" Experience the tension.

Jesus shares his inner thoughts with only his closest friends. His words bang like a hammer against their unbelieving ears. "Make fun of!" "Mock me!" "Kill!" The twelve apostles have much to think about as they trudge along in the heat. But another remark causes greater confusion: "But after three days I will come back to life again."

For these men plot against you, Lord,
but they cannot possibly succeed.
They will turn and flee
when they see your arrows
aimed straight at them.
Accept our praise, O Lord,
for all your glorious power.
We will write songs
to celebrate your mighty acts!

PSALM 21:11-13

REQUEST OF JAMES AND JOHN

Then James and John, the sons of Zebedee, came over and spoke to him in a low voice. "Master," they said, "we want you to do us a favor."

"What is it?" he asked.

"We want to sit on the thrones next to yours in your kingdom," they said, "one at your right and the other at your left!"

But Jesus answered, "You don't know what you are asking! Are you able to drink from the bitter cup of sorrow I must drink from? Or to be baptized with the baptism of suffering I must be baptized with?"

"Oh, yes," they said, "we are!"

And Jesus said, "You shall indeed drink from my cup and be baptized with my baptism, but I do not have the right to place you on thrones next to mine. Those appointments have already been made."

When the other disciples discovered what James and John had asked, they were very indignant. So Jesus called

Look into the faces of James and John—the other ten disciples. See what Jesus sees: good men but still subject to human weaknesses.

Jesus does not lecture the two disciples. He uses the occasion to teach all twelve the deep mystery of the kingdom. The "cup" (eucharist) and baptism are death-rising experiences. Each follower must share them to some extent. Jesus is the model of Christian leadership: service to others not superiority over them.

them to him and said, "As you know the kings and great men of the earth lord it over the people; but among you it is different. Whoever wants to be great among you must be your servant. And whoever wants to be greatest of all must be the slave of all. For even I, the Messiah, am not here to be served, but to help others, and to give my life as a ransom for many."

MARK 10:35-45

He lets me rest in the meadow grass
and leads me beside the quiet streams.
He restores my failing health.
He helps me do what honors him the most.
Even when walking through the dark valley
of death I will not be afraid,
for you are close beside me,
guarding, guiding all the way.

PSALM 23:3-4

HEALS BLIND BARTIMAEUS

And so they reached Jericho. Later, as they left town, a great crowd was following. Now it happened that a blind beggar named Bartimaeus (the son of Timaeus) was sitting beside the road as Jesus was going by.

When Bartimaeus heard that Jesus from Nazareth was near, he began to shout out, "Jesus, Son of David, have mercy on me!"

"Shut up!" some of the people yelled at him.

But he only shouted the louder, again and again, O Son of David, have mercy on me!"

When Jesus heard him he stopped there in the road and said, "Tell him to come here."

So they called the blind man. "You lucky fellow," they said, "come on, he's calling you!" Bartimaeus yanked off his old coat and flung it aside, jumped up and came to Jesus.

"What do you want me to do for you?" Jesus asked.

"O Teacher," the blind man said, "I want to see!"

Hear the blind man shout out to Jesus. See the people try to shut him up. Share the blind man's experience when the first sight he sees is the face of Jesus.

How many people—other than the blind man—could give a rifle-shot answer to Jesus if he asked: "What do you want me to do for you?" Then Jesus says, "Your faith has healed you." The man was physically blind but had great spiritual vision.

124

And Jesus said to him "All right, it's done. Your faith has healed you."

And instantly the blind man could see, and followed Jesus down the road!

MARK 10:46-52

In that day
the deaf will hear the words of a book,
and out of their gloom and darkness
the blind will see my plans.
The meek will be filled with fresh joy
from the Lord,
and the poor shall exult
in the Holy One of Israel.

ISAIAH 29:18-19

ENTRY INTO JERUSALEM

As they neared Bethphage and Bethany on the outskirts
of Jerusalem and came to the Mount of Olives,
Jesus sent two of his disciples on ahead.

"Go into that village over there," he told them,
"and just as you enter you will see a colt tied up that
has never been ridden. Untie him and bring him here.
And if anyone asks you what you are doing, just say,
'Our Master needs him and will return him soon.' "

Off went the two men and found the colt standing in
the street, tied outside a house. As they were untying it,
some who were standing there demanded, "What are
you doing untying that colt?"

So they said what Jesus had told them to, and
then the men agreed.

So the colt was brought to Jesus and the disciples threw
their cloaks across its back for him to ride on. Then
many in the crowd spread out their coats along the road
before him, while others threw down leafy
branches from the fields.

**See the leafy carpet being laid as a kind
of ticker-tape parade greets Jesus' arrival.
Feel the emotion that must well up within
Jesus.**

For when you die,
I will put one of your sons upon your throne
and I will make his kingdom strong.
He is the one who shall build me a temple.
And I will continue his kingdom into eternity.
I will be his father and he shall be my son.
2 SAMUEL 7:12-14

He was in the center of the procession with crowds ahead and behind, and all of them shouting, "Hail to the King!" "Praise God for him who comes in the name of the Lord!" . . . "Praise God for the return of our father David's kingdom . . ." "Hail to the King of the universe!"

And so he entered Jerusalem and went into the Temple. He looked around carefully at everything and then left—for now it was late in the afternoon—and went out to Bethany with the twelve disciples.

MARK 11:1-11

"Rejoice greatly, O my people!
Shout with joy!
For look—your King is coming!
He is the Righteous One, the Victor!
Yet he is lowly, riding on a donkey's colt!
I will disarm all peoples of the earth,
including my people in Israel,
and he shall bring peace among the nations.
His realm shall stretch from sea to sea,
from the river to the ends of the earth.

ZECHARIAH 9:9-10

THE FIG TREE CURSE

The next morning as they left Bethany, he felt hungry. A
little way off he noticed a fig tree in full leaf,
so he went over to see if he could find any figs on it.
But no, there were only leaves, for it was too early
in the season for fruit.

Then Jesus said to the tree, "You shall never bear fruit
again!" And the disciples heard him say it.

MARK 11:12-14

Five Old Testament prophets compared
Israel to a fig tree. Jesus' action becomes in-
telligible only against this prophetic tradition.
In spite of Jesus' words and works, many
people—especially the leaders—reject him.
Jesus symbolically prophesies their fate.

Woe is me!
It is hard to find an honest man
as grapes and figs
when harvest days are over.
Not a cluster to eat, not a single early fig,
however much I long for it!
The good men have disappeared from the
earth; not one fair-minded man is left.
They are all murderers,
turning against even their own brothers.

MICAH 7:1-2

And everyone shall know that it is I,
the Lord, who cuts down the high trees
and exalts the low,
that I make the green tree wither
and the dry tree grow.
I, the Lord, have said that I would do it,
and I will."

EZEKIEL 17:24

THE TEMPLE EPISODE

When they arrived back to Jerusalem he went to the Temple and began to drive out the merchants and their customers, and knocked over the tables of the moneychangers and the stalls of those selling doves, and stopped everyone from bringing in loads of merchandise.

He told them, "It is written in the Scriptures, 'My Temple is to be a place of prayer for all nations,' but you have turned it into a den of robbers."

When the chief priests and other Jewish leaders heard what he had done, they began planning how best to get rid of him. Their problem was their fear of riots because the people were so enthusiastic about Jesus' teaching.

That evening as usual they left the city.

MARK 11:15-19

The astonished onlookers recall the words of the prophet:
"Is my Temple
but a den of robbers in your eyes?
For I see all the evil going on in there."

JEREMIAH 7:11

... "And then the one you are looking for
will come suddenly to his Temple—
the Messenger of God's promises,
to bring you great joy.
Yes, he is surely coming"
says the Lord of Hosts.
"But who can live when he appears?
Who can endure his coming?
For he is like a blazing fire
refining precious metal
and he can bleach the dirtiest garments!

130

Like a refiner of silver he will sit and
closely watch as the dross is burned away.
He will purify the Levites,
the ministers of God,
refining them like gold or silver,
so that they will do their work for God
with pure hearts" . . .

MALACHI 3:1-3

The children I raised
and cared for so long and tenderly
have turned against me.
Even the animals—the donkey and the ox—
know their owner
and appreciate his care for them,
but not my people Israel.
No matter what I do for them,
they still don't care.

ISAIAH 1:2-3

THE FIG TREE LESSON

Next morning, as the disciples passed the fig tree he had cursed, they saw that it was withered from the roots! Then Peter remembered what Jesus had said to the tree on the previous day, and exclaimed, "Look, Teacher! The fig tree you cursed has withered!"

In reply Jesus said to the disciples, "If you only have faith in God—this is the absolute truth—you can say to this Mount of Olives, 'Rise up and fall into the Mediterranean,' and your command will be obeyed. All that's required is that you really believe and have no doubt! Listen to me! You can pray for *anything,* and *if you believe, you have it;* it's yours! But when you are praying, first forgive anyone you are holding a grudge against, so that your Father in heaven will forgive you your sins too."

MARK 11:20-25

The ancients lived by the sun not by the clock. Thus, Jesus and his disciples are again on the road early. Peter stops and points to the fig tree. See it standing, symbolically, in the morning freshness—dead and dried.

Jesus responds: "Listen to me!" Weigh carefully the words of Jesus that follow: faith, prayer, and forgiveness. The sermon is short in words but long in meaning. Jesus is a paradigm of what he preaches.

For the Lord says,
"Because he loves me, I will rescue him;
I will make him great
because he trusts in my name.
When he calls on me I will answer;
I will be with him in trouble,
and rescue him and honor him.
I will satisfy him with a full life
and give him my salvation."

PSALM 91:14-16

JESUS' AUTHORITY

By this time they had arrived in Jerusalem again, and as he was walking through the Temple area, the chief priests and other Jewish leaders came up to him demanding, "What's going on here? Who gave you the authority to drive out the merchants?"

Jesus replied, "I'll tell you if you answer one question! What about John the Baptist? Was he sent by God, or not? Answer me!"

They talked it over among themselves. "If we reply that God sent him, then he will say, 'All right, why didn't you accept him," But if we say God didn't send him, then the people will start a riot." (For the people all believed strongly that John was a prophet.)

So they said, "We can't answer. We don't know."

To which Jesus replied, "Then I won't answer your question either!"

MARK 11:26-33

Irate temple officials spot Jesus and his disciples. They block his way and demand to know by what right he expelled the merchants the day before.

Jesus replies with a counter-question. Recognizing the dilemma Jesus has presented for them, the officials decide to take the "5th amendment." The direction of the accusation is suddenly reversed, and the judges end up being judged.

And with a breath he can scatter
the plans of all the nations who oppose him,
but his own plan stands forever.
His intentions are the same
for every generation.
Blessed is the nation whose God is the Lord,
whose people he has chosen as his own.

PSALM 33:10-12

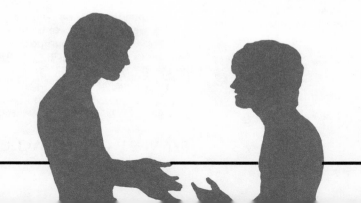

PARABLE OF THE VINEYARD TENANTS

Here are some of the story-illustrations Jesus gave to the people at that time:

"A man planted a vineyard and built a wall around it and dug a pit for pressing out the grape juice, and built a watchman's tower. Then he leased the farm to tenant farmers and moved to another country. At grape-picking time he sent one of his men to collect his share of the crop. But the farmers beat up the man and sent him back empty-handed.

"The owner then sent another of his men, who received the same treatment, only worse, for his head was seriously injured. The next man he sent was killed; and later, others were either beaten or killed, until there was only one left—his only son. He finally sent him, thinking they would surely give him their full respect.

But when the farmers saw him coming they said, 'He will own the farm when his father dies. Come on, let's kill him—and then the farm will be ours!' So they caught him and murdered him and threw his body out

After the confrontation with the temple officials, Jesus begins to teach the crowd of bystanders who have gathered. Still smarting from their unsuccessful encounter, the officials stay within earshot.

The crowd slowly begins to put together the parable. They identify the following characters in it: the planter, the vineyard, the tenant farmers, the first man, the other men, the owner's son, the new tenants. The people also saw the connection between Jesus' parable and Isaiah's Song of the Vineyard.

of the vineyard.

"What do you suppose the owner will do when he hears what happened? He will come and kill them all, and lease the vineyard to others. Don't you remember reading this verse in the Scriptures? 'The Rock the builders threw away became the cornerstone, the most honored stone in the building! This is the Lord's doing and it is an amazing thing to see.' "

The Jewish leaders wanted to arrest him then and there for using this illustration, for they knew he was pointing at them—they were the wicked farmers in his story. But they were afraid to touch him for fear of a mob. So they left him and went away.

MARK 12:1-12

Now I will sing a song about his vineyard
to the one I love.
My Beloved has a vineyard
on a very fertile hill.
He plowed it
and took out all the rocks
and planted his vineyard with the choicest
vines. He built a watchtower
and cut a winepress in the rocks.
Then he waited for the harvest,
but the grapes that grew were wild and sour
and not at all the sweet ones he expected.

ISAIAH 5:1-2

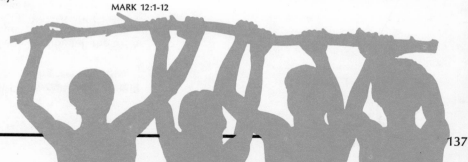

PAYING TAXES

But they sent other religious and political leaders to talk with him and try to trap him into saying something he could be arrested for.

"Teacher," these spies said, "we know you tell the truth no matter what! You aren't influenced by the opinions and desires of men, but sincerely teach the ways of God. Now tell us, is it right to pay taxes to Rome, or not?"

Jesus saw their trick and said, "Show me a coin and I'll tell you."

When they handed it to him he asked, "Whose picture and title is this on the coin?" They replied, "The emperor's."

"All right," he said, "if it is his, give it to him. But everything that belongs to God must be given to God!" And they scratched their heads in bafflement at his reply.

MARK 12:13-17

Pharisees tolerated Roman rule; Herodians opposed it. Now, they try to get Jesus to take sides. If Jesus says pay, he will be called a traitor. If he says don't, he will be reported to Rome.

All Jews especially hated the poll tax, having to pay it to Rome with silver coins bearing Caesar's "godlike" image. To possess a Roman coin was to admit a Roman obligation. Thus, Jesus asks his questioners for a coin. When they produced it, they answer their own question and expose their own trickery.

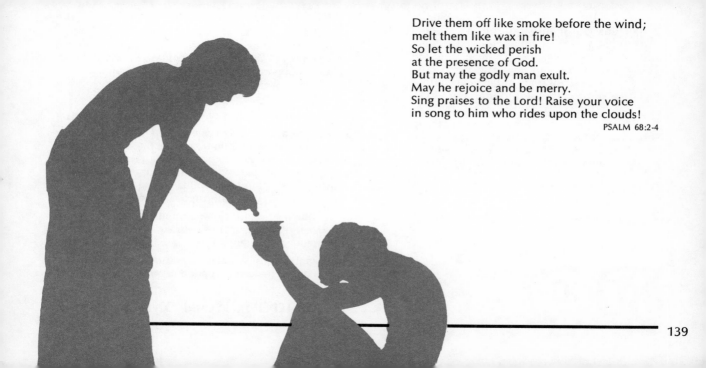

Drive them off like smoke before the wind;
melt them like wax in fire!
So let the wicked perish
at the presence of God.
But may the godly man exult.
May he rejoice and be merry.
Sing praises to the Lord! Raise your voice
in song to him who rides upon the clouds!

PSALM 68:2-4

139

ABOUT RISING FROM THE DEAD

Then the Sadducees stepped forward—a group of men who say there is no resurrection. Here was their question:

"Teacher, Moses gave us a law that when a man dies without children, the man's brother should marry his widow and have children in his brother's name.

"Well, there were seven brothers and the oldest married and died, and left no children. So the second brother married the widow but soon he died too, and left no children. Then the next brother married her, and died without children, and so on until all were dead, and still there were no children; and last of all, the woman died too.

"What we want to know is this: In the resurrection, whose wife will she be, for she had been the wife of each of them?"

Jesus replied, "Your trouble is that you don't know the Scriptures, and don't know the power of God. For when these seven brothers and the woman rise from the dead, they won't be married—they will be like the angels.

"But now as to whether there will be a resurrection—

One by one, the major religious-political groups try to discredit Jesus. Where the Pharisees and Herodians fail, the conservative Sadducees hope to succeed.

The question of the Sadducees is designed to ridicule belief in the resurrection. Jesus' answer challenges their dull way of conceiving life after death. It cannot be viewed in human, space-time terms with space-time limitations. To do this would be completely wrong.

have you never read in the book of Exodus about Moses and the burning bush? God said to Moses,'I *am* the God of Abraham, and I *am* the God of Isaac, and I *am* the God of Jacob.'

"God was telling Moses that these men, though dead for hundreds of years, were still very much alive, for he would not have said, 'I *am* the God' of those who don't exist! You have made a serious error."

MARK 12:18-27

"And many of those
whose bodies lie dead and buried
will rise up,
some to everlasting life
and some to shame
and everlasting contempt.
"And those who are wise—
the people of God—
shall shine as brightly as the sun's brillance,
and those who turn many to righteousness
will glitter like stars forever.

DANIEL 12:2-3

GREAT COMMANDMENT

One of the teachers of religion who was standing there listening to the discussion realized that Jesus had answered well. So he asked, "Of all the commandments, which is the most important?"

Jesus replied, "The one that says, 'Hear, O Israel! The Lord our God is the one and only God. And you must love him with all your heart and soul and mind and strength.'

"The second is: 'You must love others as much as yourself.' No other commandments are greater than these." The teacher of religion replied, "Sir, you have spoken a true word in saying that there is only one God and no other. And I know it is far more important to love him with all my heart and understanding and strength, and to love others as myself, than to offer all kinds of sacrifices on the altar of the Temple."

Realizing this man's understanding, Jesus said to him, "You are not far from the Kingdom of God." And after that, no one dared ask him any more questions.

MARK 12:28-34

"If you wait for your brothers to become worthy of being loved, you will wait for the rest of your life. Because they are waiting for you to love them so they can be worthy of your love. They need to be loved if they are to become better."

LOUIS EVELY

142

If anyone says "I love God,"
but keeps on hating his brother, he is a liar;
for if he doesn't love his brother
who is right there in front of him,
how can he love God
whom he has never seen?
And God himself has said
that one must love not only God,
but his brother too.

1 JOHN 4:20-21

How wonderful it is, how pleasant,
when brothers live in harmony! . . .
Harmony is as refreshing as the dew
on Mount Hermon, on the mountains of
Israel. And God has pronounced this eternal
blessing on Jerusalem, even life forevermore.

PSALM 133:1-3

143

ABOUT THE MESSIAH

Later, as Jesus was teaching the people in the Temple area, he asked them this question:

"Why do your religious teachers claim that the Messiah must be a descendant of King David? For David himself said—the Holy Spirit was speaking through him when he said it—'God said to my Lord, sit at my right hand until I make your enemies your footstool. Since David called him his Lord, how can he be his *son*?"

(This sort of reasoning delighted the crowd and they listened to him with great interest.)

MARK 12:35-37

As a boy, Jesus memorized the psalms and used them as the background of his prayer and thought. Now he quotes the first line of Psalm 110.

The context of Jesus' words is God's promise to raise up a great Messiah-king from David's line. Jews often wondered what the Messiah would be like. Jesus says the Messiah will be more than a mere son of David. His origin will be greater. Inspired by the Holy Spirit, David himself spoke of him as Lord.

144

The royal line of David will be cut off,
chopped down like a tree;
but from the stump will grow a Shoot—
yes, a new Branch from the old root.
And the Spirit of the Lord shall rest upon
him, the Spirit of wisdom, understanding,
counsel and might;
the Spirit of knowledge
and of the fear of the Lord . . .

ISAIAH 11:1-2

145

WARNING AGAINST THE LAW TEACHERS

Here are some of the other things he taught them at this time:

"Beware of the teachers of religion! For they love to wear the robes of the rich and scholarly, and to have everyone bow to them as they walk through the markets. They love to sit in the best seats in the synagogues, and at the places of honor at banquets—but they shamelessly cheat widows out of their homes and then, to cover up the kind of men they really are, they pretend to be pious by praying long prayers in public. Because of this their punishment will be the greater."

MARK 12:38-40

Jesus continues to attack religious abuse. Having addressed specific religious teaching, Jesus now confronts certain religious practices. He especially condemns outer show and the trading of large sums for long prayers.

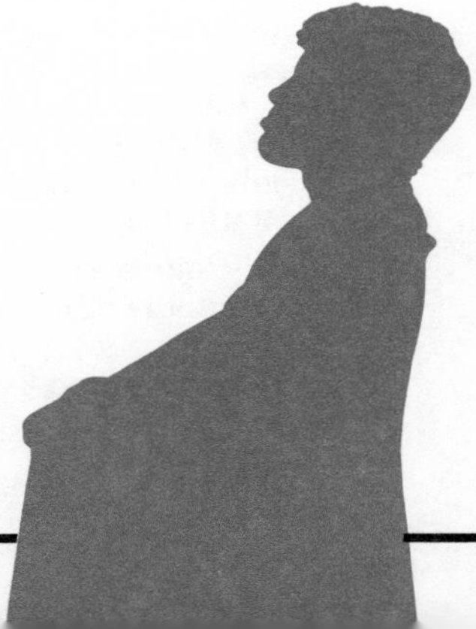

Therefore the Lord of Hosts says:
I will feed them with bitterness
and give them poison to drink.
For it is because of them
that wickedness fills this land.
This is my warning to my people,
says the Lord of Hosts.
Don't listen to these false prophets
when they prophesy to you,
filling you with futile hopes.
They are making up everything they say.
They do not speak for me!

JEREMIAH 23:15-16

I have seen their despicable acts right here
in my own Temple, says the Lord.
Therefore their paths will be dark and
slippery; they will be chased
down dark and treacherous trails, and fall.
For I will bring evil upon them and see to it,
when their time has come,
that they pay their penalty in full
for all their sins.

JEREMIAH 23:11-12

WIDOW'S OFFERING

Then he went over to the collection boxes in the Temple and sat and watched as the crowds dropped in their money. Some who were rich put in large amounts. Then a poor widow came and dropped in two pennies.

He called his disciples to him and remarked, "That poor widow has given more than all those rich men put together! For they gave a little of their extra fat, while she gave up her last penny."

MARK 12:41-44

See the thirteen trumpet-shaped offering boxes in the temple plaza. Study the people who come to give money.

Jesus notes that generosity is in the giver, not the gift. The widow's act is a patch of blue in the overcast of religious worship. Even though corruption corrodes religious leadership, true faith stays alive in the hearts of many of the people.

"The eyes of the Lord God are watching Israel, that sinful nation, and I will root her up and scatter her across the world.
Yet I have promised that this rooting out will not be permanent.

AMOS 9:8

148

JESUS SPEAKS OF THE TEMPLE

As he was leaving the Temple that day, one of his
disciples said, "Teacher, what beautiful buildings these
are! Look at the decorated stonework on the walls."
Jesus replied, "Yes, look! For not one stone will be
left upon another except as ruins."

MARK 13:1-2

The old men sit no longer in the city gates;
the young no longer dance and sing.
The joy of our hearts has ended;
our dance has turned to death.
Our glory is gone.
The crown is fallen from our head.
Woe upon us for our sins.
Our hearts are faint and weary;
our eyes grow dim.
Jerusalem and the Temple of the Lord
are desolate, deserted by all
but wild animals lurking in the ruins.

LAMENTATIONS 5:14-18

Begun to be restored about 20 B.C., the temple was still undergoing reconstruction in Jesus' day. It was the nation's greatest source of pride. But as Jesus prophecied, the Romans destroyed the temple and city in 70 A.D. Great hewn blocks of this temple are still visible in Jerusalem today.

Unless the Lord builds a house,
the builders' work is useless.
Unless the Lord protects a city,
sentries do no good.

PSALM 127:1

TROUBLES AND PERSECUTIONS

And as he sat on the slopes of the Mount of Olives across the valley from Jerusalem, Peter, James, John, and Andrew got alone with him and asked him, "Just when is all this going to happen to the Temple? Will there be some warning ahead of time?"

So Jesus launched into an extended reply. "Don't let anyone mislead you," he said, "for many will come declaring themselves to be your Messiah, and will lead many astray. And wars will break out near and far, but this is not the signal of the end-time.

"For nations and kingdoms will proclaim war against each other, and there will be earthquakes in many lands, and famines. These herald only the early stages of the anguish ahead. But when these things begin to happen, watch out! For you will be in great danger. You will be dragged before the courts, and beaten in the synagogues, and accused before governors and kings of being my followers. This is your opportunity to tell them the Good News. And the Good News must first be made known in every nation before the end-time finally comes.

Oh, what will you do
when I visit you in that day when I send
desolation upon you from a distant land?
To whom will you turn then for your help?
Where will your treasures be safe?

ISAIAH 10:3

Jesus doesn't answer the question: "Just when is all this going to happen?" He springboards to a more important crisis: the end-times. Using symbolic imagery, Jesus paints a picture of chaos: upheavals in nature, perversions of love, truth, and justice among peoples. Jesus' point is: remain faithful to the gospel and trust in God.

But when you are arrested and stand trial, don't worry about what to say in your defense. Just say what God tells you to. Then you will not be speaking, but the Holy Spirit will.

"Brothers will betray each other to death, fathers will betray their own children, and children will betray their parents to be killed. And everyone will hate you because you are mine. But all who endure to the end without renouncing me shall be saved."

MARK 13:3-13

Your power and goodness, Lord,
reach to the highest heavens.
You have done such wonderful things.
Where is there another God like you?
You have let me sink down deep
in desperate problems.
But you will bring me back to life again,
up from the depths of the earth.
You will give me greater honor than before,
and turn again and comfort me.

PSALM 71:19-21

THE AWFUL HORROR

"When you see the horrible thing standing in the Temple —reader, pay attention!—flee, if you can, to the Judean hills. Hurry! If you are on your rooftop porch, don't even go back into the house. If you are out in the fields, don't even return for your money or clothes.

"Woe to pregnant women in those days, and to mothers nursing their children. And pray that your flight will not be in winter. For those will be days of such horror as have never been since the beginning of God's creation, nor will ever be again. And unless the Lord shortens that time of calamity, not a soul in all the earth will survive. But for the sake of his chosen ones he will limit those days.

"And then if anyone tells you, 'This is the Messiah,' or, 'That one is,' don't pay any attention. For there will be many false Messiahs and false prophets who will do wonderful miracles that would deceive, if possible, even God's own children. Take care! I have warned you!"

MARK 13:14-23

Scream in terror, for the Lord's time has come, the time for the Almighty to crush you. Your arms lie paralyzed with fear; the strongest hearts melt, and are afraid. Fear grips you with terrible pangs, like those of a woman in labor. You look at one another, helpless, as the flames of the burning city reflect upon your pallid faces.

ISAIAH 13:6-8

154

Jesus returns to the topic of the destruction of the temple. The "abomination of desolation" is something akin to the statue of Zeus erected in the temple by Antiochus, when he overran and persecuted the nation in 168 B.C. Jesus' point is: flee the city rather than defend it out of some misguided messianic hope.

How the finest gold has lost its luster!
For the inlaid Temple walls are scattered
in the streets!

LAMENTATIONS 4:1

COMING OF THE SON OF MAN

"After the tribulation ends, then the sun will grow dim and the moon will not shine, and the stars will fall— the heavens will convulse.

"Then all mankind will see me, the Messiah, coming in the clouds with great power and glory. And I will send out the angels to gather together my chosen ones from all over the world—from the farthest bounds of earth and heaven."

MARK 13:24-27

The heavens will be black above them.
No light will shine from stars or sun or moon.

ISAIAH 13:10

The turmoil in nature and the distortion of truth, love, and justice in people—these are the birth pangs ushering in the fulfillment of God's kingdom. Then the Son of Man will return in power and glory to reign forever.

He will wipe away all tears from their eyes,
and there shall be no more death,
nor sorrow, nor crying, nor pain.
And the one sitting on the throne said,
"See, I am making all things new!"

REVELATION 21:4-5

156

LESSON OF THE FIG TREE

"Now, here is a lesson from a fig tree. When its buds become tender and its leaves begin to sprout, you know that spring has come. And when you see these things happening that I've described, you can be sure that my return is very near that I am right at the door.

"Yes, these are the events that will signal the end of the age. Heaven and earth shall disappear, but my words stand sure forever."

MARK 13:28-31

See Jesus stop and touch the branch of a budding fig tree. Hear the seriousness of his words. Feel what the apostles feel at this moment.

Jesus is saying that God speaks to us through the events of daily life and history. They have a deeper meaning than the surface one. They are like undeveloped negatives that need light to expose their hidden meaning. Jesus' teaching is that light. We must learn to decipher God's Word in the events of our daily lives and history.

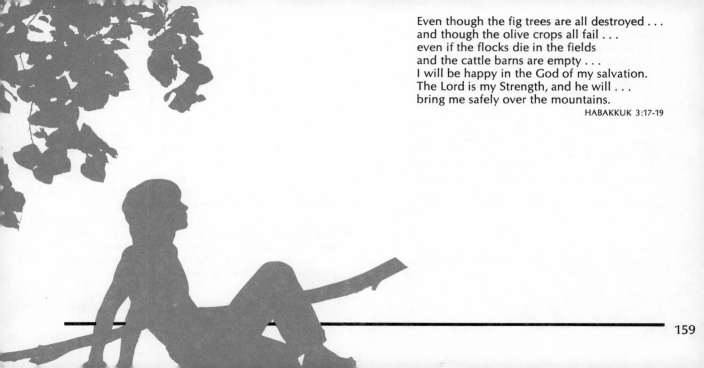

Even though the fig trees are all destroyed . . .
and though the olive crops all fail . . .
even if the flocks die in the fields
and the cattle barns are empty . . .
I will be happy in the God of my salvation.
The Lord is my Strength, and he will . . .
bring me safely over the mountains.

HABAKKUK 3:17-19

WHO KNOWS THE HOUR

"However, no one, not even the angels in heaven, nor I myself, knows the day or hour when these things will happen; only the Father knows. And since you don't know when it will happen, stay alert. Be on the watch (for my return).

"My coming can be compared with that of a man who went on a trip to another country. He laid out his employees' work for them to do while he was gone, and told the gatekeeper to watch for his return.

"Keep a sharp lookout! For you do not know when I will come, at evening, at midnight, early dawn or late daybreak. Don't let me find you sleeping. *Watch for my return!* This is my message to you and to everyone else."

MARK 13:32-37

As Jesus speaks, the people remember the frightening words of Isaiah:
"When the Lord stands up from his throne
to shake up the earth,
his enemies will crawl with fear
into the holes in the rocks and into the caves
. . . to try to get away from the terror of the
Lord and the glory of his majesty
when he rises to terrify the earth."

ISAIAH 2:19, 21

The hour of his coming lies hidden. The world ends for everyone when his own life ends. What that hour brings for each depends upon what each brings to it.

With this news
bring cheer to all discouraged ones.
Encourage those who are afraid.
Tell them,
"Be strong, fear not, for your God is coming
to destroy your enemies.
He is coming to save you."

ISAIAH 35:3-4

161

PLOT AGAINST JESUS

The passover observance began two days later—an annual Jewish holiday when no bread made with yeast was eaten. The chief priests and other Jewish leaders were still looking for an opportunity to arrest Jesus secretly and put him to death.

"But we can't do it during the Passover," they said, "or there will be a riot."

MARK 14:1-2

See Jews pouring into Jerusalem from small towns to celebrate the week-long feast of the Passover. Share the excitement. Sense the hostility mounting against Jesus in priestly circles.

The Passover celebrated the "passing-over" of ancient Jews from slavery in Egypt to freedom as God's chosen people at Mount Sinai. It began the evening before with the slaughter of sacrificial lambs in the temple. Jesus undoubtedly thought about all this as he walked toward Jerusalem with his friends.

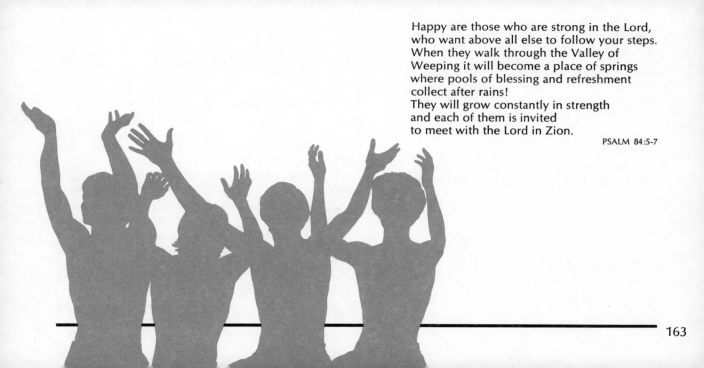

Happy are those who are strong in the Lord,
who want above all else to follow your steps.
When they walk through the Valley of
Weeping it will become a place of springs
where pools of blessing and refreshment
collect after rains!
They will grow constantly in strength
and each of them is invited
to meet with the Lord in Zion.

PSALM 84:5-7

163

ANOINTED AT BETHANY

Meanwhile Jesus was in Bethany, at the home of Simon the leper; during supper a woman came in with a beautiful flask of expensive perfume. Then, breaking the seal, she poured it over his head.

Some of those at the table were indignant among themselves about this "waste," as they called it.

"Why, she could have sold that perfume for a fortune and given the money to the poor!" they snarled.

But Jesus said, "Let her alone; why berate her for doing a good thing? You always have the poor among you, and they badly need your help, and you can aid them whenever you want to; but I won't be here much longer.

"She has done what she could, and has anointed my body ahead of time for burial. And I tell you this in solemn truth, that wherever the Good News is preached throughout the world, this woman's deed will be remembered and praised."

MARK 14:3-9

The table talk about the holiday halts suddenly. An unannounced woman enters to express her feelings toward Jesus. The fragrance of the oil tells everyone that it is expensive.

The word "Messiah" means "the anointed one" in English. In Greek, it is translated "the Christ." The deeper meaning of the anointing is missed by many who criticize the woman harshly. Operating from intuitive love rather than business logic, the woman had performed a deep symbolic action. No one would forget it, least of all Jesus.

You provide delicious food for me
in the presence of my enemies.
You have welcomed me as your guest;
blessings overflow!

PSALM 23:5

BETRAYAL OF JESUS

Then Judas Iscariot, one of his disciples, went to the chief priests to arrange to betray Jesus to them.

When the chief priests heard why he had come, they were excited and happy and promised him a reward. So he began looking for the right time and place to betray Jesus.

MARK 14:10-11

"Everytime I look at you I don't understand why you let the things you did get so out of hand. You'd have managed better if you'd planned."

JUDAS IN *JESUS CHRIST SUPERSTAR*

Was Judas disillusioned? Was he aware of what the others were not aware of: that Jesus was headed for death? Did he feel that Jesus had bungled a great chance to gain a position of power in the Jewish community and to help the people in a practical way?

This plan of mine
is not what you would work out,
neither are my thoughts the same as yours!
For just as the heavens are higher than the
earth, so are my ways higher than yours,
and my thoughts than yours.

ISAIAH 55:8-9

EATING WITH HIS DISCIPLES

On the first day of the Passover, the day the lambs were sacrificed, his disciples asked him where he wanted to go to eat the traditional Passover supper. He sent two of them into Jerusalem to make the arrangements.

"As you are walking along," he told them, "you will see a man coming towards you carrying a pot of water. Follow him. At the house he enters, tell the man in charge, 'Our Master sent us to see the room you have ready for us, where we will eat the Passover supper this evening!' He will take you upstairs to a large room all set up. Prepare our supper there."

So the two disciples went on ahead into the city and found everything as Jesus had said, and prepared the Passover.

In the evening Jesus arrived with the other disciples, and as they were sitting around the table eating, Jesus said, "I solemnly declare that one of you will betray me, one of you who is here eating with me."

A great sadness swept over them, and one by one they

With the disciples, search the crowded city streets for the man carrying a pot of water. When you find him, talk with him; go with him to the Supper Room.

Join Jesus and the disciples at the table in the candle-lit room. Smell the food and feel the mood shift from joy to confusion when Jesus says: "One of you will betray me." Hear Jesus say: "I must die as the prophets declared long ago."

asked him, "Am I the one?"

He replied, "It is one of you twelve eating with me now.
I must die, as the prophets declared long ago; but,
oh, the misery ahead for the man by whom I am betrayed.
Oh, that he had never been born!"

MARK 14:12-21

He was oppressed and he was afflicted,
yet he never said a word.
He was brought as a lamb to the slaughter;
and as a sheep before her shearers is dumb,
so he stood silent
before the ones condemning him . . .

ISAIAH 53:7

LORD'S SUPPER

As they were eating, Jesus took bread and asked God's blessing on it and broke it in pieces and gave it to them and said, "Eat it—this is my body."

Then he took a cup of wine and gave thanks to God for it and gave it to them; and they all drank from it. And he said to them, "This is my blood, poured out for many, sealing the new agreement between God and man. I solemnly declare that I shall never again taste wine until the day I drink a different kind in the Kingdom of God."

Then they sang a hymn and went out to the Mount of Olives.

MARK 14:22-26

Sit with Jesus and the apostles around the table. Look into each weather-beaten face. Go beyond the face to the thoughts in the minds of each—especially Jesus.

For Jews, to drink from another's cup was to share his fate. To eat his bread was to share his blessing. This is what happens. Jesus and his disciples forge a new covenant. Those who drink of the cup and eat of the bread share forever the fate and blessing of Jesus. They "covenant" with him.

170

I want to go wherever you go,
and live wherever you live;
your people shall be my people,
and your God shall be my God;
I want to die where you die,
and be buried there.

RUTH 1:16-17

171

PREDICTS PETER'S DENIAL

"All of you will desert me," Jesus told them, "for God has declared through the prophets, 'I will kill the Shepherd, and the sheep will scatter,' But after I am raised to life again, I will go to Galilee and meet you there."

Peter said to him, "I will never desert you no matter what the others do!"

"Peter," Jesus said, "before the cock crows a second time tomorrow morning you will deny me three times."

"No!" Peter exploded. "Not even if I have to die with you! I'll *never* deny you!" And all the others vowed the same.

MARK 14:27-31

Feel the sting of Jesus' words hit the ears of Peter. Share Peter's intense determination as he reaffirms his loyalty to Jesus.

The disciples must be reminded of the prophecies in the Old Testament. They had read them often but had not fully understood what they read. Will the disciples flee from fear or because of a sudden loss of faith? Left to himself, man is always a victim—never a victor.

172

. . . Strike down the Shepherd
and the sheep will scatter,
but I will come back
and comfort and care
for the lambs . . .
I will bring the third that remain
through the fire and make them pure,
as gold and silver are refined and purified
by fire.

ZECHARIAH 13:7, 9

173

PRAYS IN GETHSEMANE

And now they came to an olive grove called the Garden of Gethsemane, and he instructed his disciples "Sit here, while I go and pray."

He took Peter, James and John with him and began to be filled with horror and deepest distress. And he said to them, "My soul is crushed by sorrow to the point of death; stay here and watch with me."

He went on a little further and fell to the ground and prayed that if it were possible the awful hour awaiting him might never come.

"Father, Father," he said, "everything is possible for you. Take away this cup from me. Yet I want your will, not mine."

Then he returned to the three disciples and found them asleep.

"Simon!" he said. "Asleep? Couldn't you watch with me even one hour? Watch with me and pray lest the Tempter overpower you. For though the spirit is willing enough, the body is weak."

See the lights of Jerusalem across the valley. What makes Jesus go off by himself into the night? Share the disciples' feelings each time Jesus returns to wake them.

Newspaperman Hugh Kay said to a young man having faith problems:
"The darkness you are encountering is in itself a rich experience. If it be that you really want to meet Our Lord, then it is by moonlight that you must seek Him under an olive tree. You will find Him flat on the ground, and you will have to lie down on your face with Him if you are to catch His words."

And he went away again and prayed, repeating his pleadings. Again he returned to them and found them sleeping, for they were very tired. And they didn't know what to say.

The third time when he returned to them he said, "Sleep on; get your rest! But no! The time for sleep has ended! Look! I am betrayed into the hands of wicked men. Come! Get up! We must go! Look! My betrayer is here!"

MARK 14:32-42

I am in deep trouble
and I need his help so badly.
All night long I pray,
lifting my hands to heaven, pleading.
I think of God and moan,
overwhelmed with longing for his help.
I cannot sleep . . .
I am too distressed even to pray.

PSALM 77:2-4

ARREST OF JESUS

And immediately, while he was still speaking, Judas (one of his disciples) arrived with a mob equipped with swords and clubs, sent out by the chief priests and other Jewish leaders.

Judas had told them, "You will know which one to arrest when I go over and greet him. Then you can take him easily." So as soon as they arrived he walked up to Jesus. "Master!" he exclaimed, and embraced him with a great show of friendliness. Then the mob arrested Jesus and held him fast. But someone pulled a sword and slashed at the High Priest's servant, cutting off his ear.

Jesus asked them, "Am I some dangerous robber, that you come like this, armed to the teeth to capture me? Why didn't you arrest me in the Temple? I was there teaching every day. But these things are happening to fulfill the prophecies about me."

Meanwhile, all his disciples had fled. There was, however, a young man following along behind, clothed only in a linen nightshirt. When the mob tried to grab him, he

See the swinging lanterns and the angry mob. Hear the shouts of profanity. Feel the cold greeting of Judas. Taste the fright of the fleeting youth. Enter into the mind and heart of Jesus.

This friend of mine betrayed me—
I who was at peace with him.
He broke his promises . . .
His words were sweet,
but underneath were daggers.

PSALM 54:20-21

Because the Lord God helps me,
I will not be dismayed;
therefore, I set my face like flint
to do his will,
and I know that I will triumph.

ISAIAH 50:7 176

escaped, though his clothes were torn off in the process,
so that he ran away completely naked.

MARK 14:43-52

BEFORE THE COUNCIL

Jesus was led to the High Priest's home where all of the chief priests and other Jewish leaders soon gathered. Peter followed far behind and then slipped inside the gates of the High Priest's residence and crouched beside a fire among the servants.

Inside, the chief priests and the whole Jewish Supreme Court were trying to find something against Jesus that would be sufficient to condemn him to death. But their efforts were in vain. Many false witnesses volunteered, but they contradicted each other.

Finally some men stood up to lie about him and said, "We heard him say, 'I will destroy this Temple made with human hands and in three days I will build another, made without human hands!' " But even then they didn't get their stories straight!

Then the High Priest stood up before the Court and asked Jesus, "Do you refuse to answer this charge? What do you have to say for yourself?"

To this Jesus made no reply.

They have no reason to hate and fight me,
yet they do!
I love them,
but even while I am praying for them,
they are trying to destroy me.
They return evil for good,
and hatred for love.

PSALM 109:3-5

Jesus leaves no doubt when asked: "Are you the Messiah, the Son of God?" He affirms it and cites Daniel 7:14. The high priest leaves no doubt that he understands Jesus' answer. He tore his robes, a sign to protest Jesus' claim.

178

Then the High Priest asked him. "Are you the Messiah, the Son of God?"

Jesus said, "I am, and you will see me sitting at the right hand of God, and returning to earth in the clouds of heaven."

Then the High Priest tore at his clothes and said, "What more do we need? Why wait for witnesses? You have heard his blasphemy. What is your verdict?" And the vote for the death sentence was unanimous.

Then some of them began to spit at him, and they blindfolded him and began to hammer his face with their fists.

"Who hit you that time, you prophet?" they jeered. And even the bailiffs were using their fists on him as they led him away.

MARK 14:53-65

But, oh, how few believed it!
Who will listen? . . .
We despised him and rejected him—
a man of sorrows,
acquainted with bitterest grief.
We turned our backs on him
and looked the other way when he went by.
He was despised and we didn't care.

ISAIAH 53:1, 3

DENIES JESUS

Meanwhile Peter was below in the courtyard. One of the maids who worked for the High Priest noticed Peter warming himself at the fire.

She looked at him closely and then announced, "*You were with Jesus, the Nazarene.*"

Peter denied it. "I don't know what you're talking about!" he said, and walked over to the edge of the courtyard.

Just then, a rooster crowed.

The maid saw him standing there and began telling the others, "There he is! There's that disciple of Jesus!"

Peter denied it again.

A little later others standing around the fire began saying to Peter, "You are, too, one of them, for you are from Galilee!"

He began to curse and swear. "I don't even know this fellow you are talking about," he said.

And immediately the rooster crowed the second time.

It was not an enemy who taunted me—
then I could have borne it;
I could have hidden and escaped.
But it was you, a man like myself,
my companion and my friend.

PSALM 55:12-13

Peter's three denials gradually worsen: feigned ignorance, simple denial, a sworn oath of denial. This is the same Peter who said: "I will never desert you no matter what the others do!" Man does not know the capacity for evil within him.

Even my best friend has turned against me—
a man I completely trusted;
how often we ate together.

PSALM 41:9

Suddenly Jesus' words flashed through Peter's mind:
"Before the cock crows twice, you will deny me three
times." And he began to cry.

MARK 14:66-72

BEFORE PILATE

Early in the morning the chief priests, elders and teachers of religion—the entire Supreme Court—met to discuss their next steps. Their decision was to send Jesus under guard to Pilate, the Roman governor.

Pilate asked him, "Are you the King of the Jews?"

"Yes," Jesus replied, "it is as you say."

Then the chief priests accused him of many crimes, and Pilate asked him, "Why don't you say something? What about all these charges against you?"

But Jesus said no more, much to Pilate's amazement.

MARK 15:1-5

Crude chains gnaw at Jesus' wrists as he is led like an animal through the cobblestone streets. The last day of Jesus' dwelling among men begins.

Jesus responds only to Pilate's question of kingship. To the "many crimes" of which he is accused, Jesus responds with silence. Pilate is amazed. Prisoners usually answer their accusers with denials—and obscenities. What kind of prisoner is this, anyway?

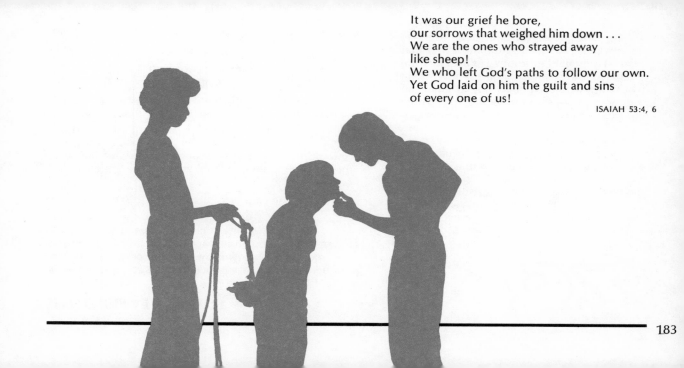

It was our grief he bore,
our sorrows that weighed him down . . .
We are the ones who strayed away
like sheep!
We who left God's paths to follow our own.
Yet God laid on him the guilt and sins
of every one of us!

ISAIAH 53:4, 6

183

SENTENCED TO DEATH

Now, it was Pilate's custom to release one Jewish prisoner each year at Passover time—any prisoner the people requested. One of the prisoners at that time was Barabbas, convicted along with others for murder during an insurrection.

Now a mob began to crowd in toward Pilate, asking him to release a prisoner as usual.

"How about giving you the 'King of Jews'?" Pilate asked. "Is he the one you want released?" (For he realized by now that this was a frameup, backed by the chief priests because they envied Jesus' popularity.)

But at this point the chief priests whipped up the mob to demand the release of Barabbas instead of Jesus.

"But if I release Barabbas," Pilate asked them, "what shall I do with this man you call your king?"

They shouted back, "Crucify him!"

"But why?" Pilate demanded. "What has he done wrong?" They only roared the louder, "Crucify him!"

I didn't know
that they were planning to kill me!
"Let's destroy this man and all his messages,"
they said.
"Let's kill him so that his name will be forever
forgotten."

JEREMIAH 11:19

Pressured by the chief priests and the crowd, Pilate compromises — Choose one: the rebel or the king. To please the crowd, Pilate releases the criminal and condemns Jesus. Pilate's pattern of action has been repeated many times by many men: external pressure bends personal conviction. Right is crucified by wrong.

Then Pilate, afraid of a riot and anxious to please the people, released Barabbas to them. And he ordered Jesus flogged with a leaded whip, and handed him over to be crucified.

MARK 15:6-15

Everyone who sees me
mocks and sneers and shrugs.
"Is this the one
who rolled his burden on the Lord?"
they laugh. "Is this the one
who claims the Lord delights in him?
We'll believe it when we see
God rescue him!"

PSALM 22:7-8

SOLDIERS MOCK JESUS

Then the Roman soldiers took him into the barracks
of the palace, called out the entire palace guard, dressed
him in a purple robe, and made a crown of long,
sharp thorns and put it on his head. Then they saluted,
yelling, "Yea! King of the Jews!" And they beat him on
the head with a cane, and spit on him and went down
on their knees to "worship" him.

When they finally tired of their sport, they took off the
purple robe and put his own clothes on him again,
and led him away to be crucified.

MARK 15:16-20

I am a worm, not a man,
scorned and despised by my own people
and by all mankind.

PSALM 22:6

I give my back to the whip,
and my cheeks
to those who pull out the beard.
I do not hide from shame—
they spit in my face.

ISAIAH 50:6

But he was wounded and bruised for *our* sins.
He was chastised that we might have peace;
he was lashed—and we were healed!
We are the ones
who strayed away like sheep!
We, who left God's path to follow our own.
Yet God laid on *him*
the guilt and sins of every one of us!
He was oppressed and he was afflicted,
yet he never said a word.
He was brought as a lamb to the slaughter;
and as a sheep before her shearers is dumb,
so he stood silent
before the ones condemning him.

ISAIAH 53:5-7

NAILED TO THE CROSS

Simon of Cyrene, who was coming in from the country just then, was pressed into service to carry Jesus' cross. (Simon is the father of Alexander and Rufus.)

And they brought Jesus to a place called Golgotha. (Golgotha means skull.) Wine drugged with bitter herbs was offered to him there, but he refused it. And then they crucified him—and threw dice for his clothes.

It was about nine o'clock in the morning when the crucifixion took place.

A signboard was fastened to the cross above his head, announcing his crime. It read, "The King of the Jews."

Two robbers were also crucified that morning, their crosses on either side of his. And so the Scripture was fulfilled that said, "He was counted among evil men."

The people jeered at him as they walked by, and wagged their heads in mockery.

"Ha! Look at you now!" they yelled at him. "Sure, you can destroy the Temple and rebuild it in three days!

Their contempt has broken my heart;
my spirit is heavy within me.
If even one would show some pity,
if even one would comfort me!
For food they gave me poison;
for my awful thirst they offered me vinegar.

PSALM 69:20-21

My strength has dried up like sun-baked clay;
my tongue sticks to my mouth,
for you have laid me in the dust of death.
The enemy, this gang of evil men, circles me
like a pack of dogs;
they have pierced my hands and feet.
I can count every bone in my body.
See these men of evil gloat and stare;
they divide my clothes among themselves
by a toss of the dice.

PSALM 22:15-18

If you're so wonderful, save yourself and come down from the cross."

The chief priests and religious leaders were also standing around joking about Jesus.

"He's quite clever at 'saving' others," they said, "but he can't save himself!"

"Hey there, Messiah!" they yelled at him. "You 'King of Israel'! Come on down from the cross and we'll believe you!"

And even the two robbers dying with him, cursed him.

MARK 15:21-32

Who among the people of that day
realized it was their sins
that he was dying for—
that he was suffering their punishment.

ISAIAH 53:8

189

DEATH OF JESUS

About noon, darkness fell across the entire land,
lasting until three o'clock that afternoon.

Then Jesus called out with a loud voice, "Eli, Eli, lama
sabachthani?" ("My God, my God, why have
you deserted me?")

Some of the people standing there thought he was
calling for the prophet Elijah. So one man ran and got a
sponge and filled it with sour wine and held it up
to him on a stick.

"Let's see if Elijah will come and take him down!" he said.

Then Jesus uttered another loud cry, and dismissed
his spirit.

And the curtain in the Temple was split apart from
top to bottom.

When the Roman officer standing beside his cross saw
how he dismissed his spirit, he exclaimed, "Truly,
this was the Son of God!"

Some women were there watching from a distance—

My God, my God, why have you forsaken me?
Why do you refuse to help me
or even to listen to my groans? . . .
My strength has drained away like water,
and all my bones are out of joint.
My heart melts like wax.

PSALM 22:1, 14

For centuries the Jerusalem temple sym-
bolized God's presence among his people.
The tearing of the curtain symbolizes God's
departure from the temple. The Old Testament and sacrifice are now ended. A new
temple and a new sacrifice are inaugurated
by Jesus.

Mary Magdalene, Mary (the mother of James the Younger and of Joses), Salome, and others. They and many other Galilean women who were his followers had ministered to him when he was up in Galilee, and had come with him to Jerusalem.

MARK 15:33-41

I couldn't rest, I couldn't sleep, thinking how
I ought to build a permanent home
for the Ark of the Lord,
a Temple for the mighty one of Israel.
Then I vowed that I would do it;
I made a solemn promise to the Lord.

PSALM 132:3-5

BURIAL OF JESUS

This all happened the day before the Sabbath. Late that afternoon Joseph from Arimathea, an honored member of the Jewish Supreme Court (who personally was eagerly expecting the arrival of God's Kingdom), gathered his courage and went to Pilate and asked for Jesus' body.

Pilate couldn't believe that Jesus was already dead so he called for the Roman officer in charge and asked him. The officer confirmed the fact, and Pilate told Joseph he could have the body.

Joseph bought a long sheet of linen cloth and, taking Jesus' body down from the cross, wound it in the cloth and laid it in a rock-hewn tomb, and rolled a stone in front of the entrance.

(Mary Magdalene and Mary the mother of Joses were watching as Jesus was laid away.)

MARK 15:42-47

Stand with Jesus' mother at the tomb. Share her sorrow. Speak to her from your heart.

He was buried like a criminal
in a rich man's grave;
but he had done no wrong,
and had never spoken an evil word.

ISAIAH 53:9

I think of God and moan,
overwhelmed with longing for his help . . .
And I said: This is my fate,
that the blessings of God have changed
to hate.
I recall the many miracles he did for me
so long ago.
Those wonderful deeds
are constantly in my thoughts.
I cannot stop thinking about them.

PSALM 77:3, 10-12

RESURRECTION

The next evening, when the Sabbath ended, Mary Magdalene and Salome and Mary, the mother of James, went out and purchased embalming spices.

Early the following morning, just at sunrise, they carried them out to the tomb. On the way they were discussing how they could ever roll aside the huge stone from the entrance.

But when they arrived they looked up and saw that the stone—a *very* heavy one—was already moved away and the entrance was open! So they entered the tomb—and there on the right sat a young man clothed in white. The women were startled, but the angel said, "Don't be so surprised. Aren't you looking for Jesus, the Nazarene who was crucified? He isn't here! He has come back to life! Look, that's where his body was lying. Now go and give this message to his disciples including Peter:

" 'Jesus is going ahead of you to Galilee. You will see him there, just as he told you before he died!' "

O Lord my God, I pleaded with you,
and you gave me my health again.
You brought me back
from the brink of the grave,
from death itself,
and here I am alive!

PSALM 30:2-3

The stone rejected by the builders
has now become the capstone of the arch!
This is the Lord's doing,
and it is marvelous to see!
This is the day the Lord has made.
We will rejoice and be glad in it.

PSALM 118:22-24

The women fled from the tomb, trembling and bewildered, too frightened to talk.

MARK 16:1-8

In my discouragement I thought,
"They are lying when they say I will recover."
But now what can I offer . . .
for all he has done for me?

PSALM 116:10-12

APPEARS TO MARY MAGDALENE

It was early on Sunday morning when Jesus came back to life, and the first person who saw him was Mary Magdalene—the woman from whom he had cast out seven demons. She found the disciples wet-eyed with grief and exclaimed that she had seen Jesus, and he was alive! But they didn't believe her!

MARK 16:9-11

"The best thing about the resurrection of Christ is that the apostles were the last to admit it. When the first reports came . . . they thought it was 'madness' and therefore 'would not believe.' "

JOSEPH MANTON

Then he turned my sorrow into joy!
He took away my clothes of mourning
and gave me gay and festive garments
to rejoice in so that I might sing
glad praises to the Lord
instead of lying in silence in the grave.
O Lord my God,
I will keep on thanking you forever!

PSALM 30:11-12

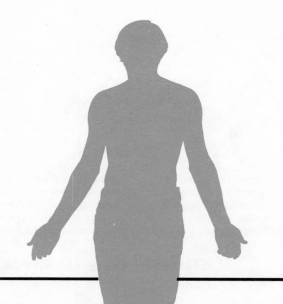

For the lamb standing in front
of the throne will feed them
and be their Shepherd
and lead them to the springs
of the Water of Life.
And God will wipe their tears away.

REVELATION 7:17

APPEARS TO TWO DISCIPLES

Later that day he appeared to two who were walking from
Jerusalem into the country, but they didn't recognize
him at first because he had changed his appearance.
When they finally realized who he was, they rushed back
to Jerusalem to tell the others, but no one believed them.

MARK 16:12-13

When I saw him, I fell at his feet as dead;
but he laid his right hand one me and said,
"Don't be afraid!
Though I am the First and Last,
the Living One who died,
who is now alive forevermore,
who has the keys of hell and death—
don't be afraid!"

REVELATION 1:17-18

"They all had heard Christ say, 'I have the
power to lay down my life and to take it up
again' . . . But they were peasants, they were
Galileans, they were dull-witted."

JOSEPH MANTON

His anger lasts a moment;
his favors lasts for life!
Weeping may go on all night,
but in the morning there is joy.

PSALM 30:5

APPEARS TO THE ELEVEN

Still later he appeared to the eleven disciples as they were eating together. He rebuked them for their unbelief —their stubborn refusal to believe those who had seen him alive from the dead.

And then he told them, "You are to go into all the world and preach the Good News to everyone, everywhere. Those who believe and are baptized will be saved. But those who refuse to believe will be condemned.

"And those who believe shall use my authority to cast out demons, and they shall speak new languages. They will be able even to handle snakes with safety, and if they drink anything poisonous, it won't hurt them; and they will be able to place their hands on the sick and heal them."

MARK 16:14-18

Look deeply into the faces of the eleven disciples: Peter who denied Jesus, John who stood beneath the cross, the rest who fled. Read their thoughts.

"From that time on, the men of Palestine who had been Christ's followers never wavered from the faith. They were totally convinced that Jesus Christ was the Messiah and he had indeed cheated death . . . Off they went with burning urgency to tell the news to all the world . . . Their lives were led for that end, and for that end alone. No amount of persecution could stop them."

F. B. RHEIN

This is the Lord's doing,
and it is marvelous to see!
This is the day the Lord has made.
We will rejoice and be glad in it!

PSALM 118:23-24

JESUS IS TAKEN UP TO HEAVEN

When the Lord Jesus had finished talking with them, he was taken up into heaven and sat down at God's right hand.

And the disciples went everywhere preaching, and the Lord was with them and confirmed what they said by the miracles that followed their messages.

MARK 16:19-20

"And if his resurrection isn't just a dream for dying men, then he's the one who has to come and bring this globe to life again."
NORMAN HABEL

"The lives and message of these men changed the course of human history. No reasonable explanation has ever been given to account for their transformed lives except their own: they had seen Jesus alive . . ."
ROBERT CLEATH

"See, I am coming soon,
and my reward is with me, to repay everyone
according to the deeds he has done.
I am the A and the Z,
the Beginning and the End,
the First and Last.

REVELATION 22:12-13